DIRECTIONS IN DEVELOPMENT

Building a Sustainable Future
The Africa Region Environment Strategy

THE WORLD BANK
Washington, D.C.

Cover photo credits:
    Foreground—Agi Kiss, World Bank.
    Background—Robert Clement-Jones, World Bank.

Library of Congress Cataloging-in-Publication Data

Building a sustainable future : the Africa region environment strategy,
        p. cm. — (directions in development)
    Includes bibliographical references.
    ISBN 0-8213-5146-X
    1. Sustainable development—Africa. 2. Environmental policy—Economic
aspects—Africa. 3. Natural resources—Africa—Management. 4. World Bank—
Africa.   I. Series.

HC800.Z9 E513 2002
338.96'07—dc21

2002069155

Contents

Foreword

Better environmental management is a matter of survival. In Africa and around the world, this simple truth has never been better appreciated than it is today. One of the eight global Millennium Development Goals for improving the lives of the world's poor calls for reversing current trends in the loss of environmental resources. The Environmental Initiative of the New Partnership for African Development, Africa's revival plan, identifies urgent actions needed for better management of land, water, and biological resources as well as for the strengthening of environmental governance and financing. The message also resonates in the World Bank's mission statement: "To fight poverty with passion and professionalism for lasting results; to help people help themselves and their environment."

African governments and people are committed to reducing poverty in the region through economic growth and development that are both inclusive and sustainable. Among the greatest challenges they face in achieving this goal is sustaining and developing the human and natural capital that provides the foundation for growth. This environment strategy for the Africa Region articulates the World Bank's commitment to help African countries make the transition to sustainable economic development through improved management of natural resources and the environment. It calls for a supportive government (through wise policies and regulations), informed and empowered communities, and a dynamic and well-guided private sector to work together, and for the Bank and others to help provide the necessary knowledge base, capacity development, and financial resources.

In the year that the Republic of South Africa is hosting the World Summit on Sustainable Development, we appreciate that the African people can and must be active and equal partners in the quest to define and build a more sustainable future for themselves and for us all.

Preface

This environment strategy outlines the current thinking in the World Bank Group Africa Region about priorities and actions for the institution in the environmental arena. It benefited from extensive consultations with the Bank's clients and partners, who contributed valuable insights and recommendations. However, the final contents and presentation are the responsibility of the World Bank's Africa Region staff and management. The successful implementation of the strategy will depend on demand by borrowing countries, cooperation by development partners including civil society, and the availability of financial resources. Throughout this volume, "Africa" refers to Sub-Saharan Africa. In the World Bank's institutional structure, North African countries fall within the Middle East and North Africa (MENA) region.

Abbreviations and Acronyms

AFTES	Africa Region Environment and Social Development Unit
ALWMI	African Land and Water Management Initiative
AMCEN	African Ministerial Conference on Environment
APL	Adaptable Program Loan
ARES	Africa Region Environment Strategy
ASAL	Arid and semi-arid lands
ASP	Africa Stockpile Program
CAP	Community Action Plan or Program
CAS	Country Assistance Strategy
CBNRM	Community-Based Natural Resource Management
CDD	Community-Driven Development
CDF	Comprehensive Development Framework
CEPF	Critical Ecosystems Partnership Fund
CILSS	Permanent Interstate Committee for Drought Control in the Sahel
CITES	Convention on the International Trade in Endangered Species
DRC	Democratic Republic of Congo
DRE	Decentralized rural electrification
EA	Environmental Assessment
EACC	East African Cooperation Community
ECOWAS	Economic Community of West African States
EIA	Environmental Impact Assessment
EMP	Environmental Management Plan
ESP	Environmental Support Program
ESW	Economic and sector work
GDP	Gross domestic product
GEF	Global Environment Facility
GIS	Geographic Information System
GNP	Gross national product
ICZM	Integrated Coastal Zone Management

IDA	International Development Association
IEM	Integrated Ecosystem Management
IGADD	Intergovernmental Authority on Drought and Development
ILWMAP	Integrated Land-Water Management Action Program in Africa
IPM	Integrated Pest Management
JOS	Joint Operational Strategy for Biodiversity Conservation and Improved Forest Management
MDG	Millennium Development Goals
MELISSA	Managing Environment Locally in Sub-Saharan Africa
NBCSPs	National Biodiversity Conservation Strategies and Plans
NDF	Nordic Development Fund
NEAP	National Environmental Action Plan
NEPAD	New Partnership for African Development
NESDA	Network for Environment and Sustainable Development in Africa
NGO	Nongovernmental organization
PAGE	Pilot Assessment of Global Ecosystems
PERC	Public Expenditure Review Credit
PRA	Participatory Rural Appraisal
PRSC	Poverty Reduction Strategy Credit
PRSP	Poverty Reduction Strategy Paper
RD	Rural development
REIMP	Central African Regional Environmental Information Management Program
RESA	Renewable (Nontraditional) Energy Strategy for Africa
SADC	Southern Africa Development Community
SAIEA	South African Institute of Environmental Assessment
SAL	Structural Adjustment Loan
SEA	Strategic or "Sectoral" Environmental Assessment
SP	Safeguard Policy
TM	Traditional medicine
UNDP	United Nations Development Programme
UNEP	United Nations Environment Programme
VPU	Vice Presidential Unit (World Bank)
WAEN	West African Enterprise Network
WBES	World Bank Environment Strategy
WRI	World Resources Institute

Executive Summary

In Africa, specifically Sub-Saharan Africa, the World Bank's mission to fight poverty with lasting results is inescapably linked with environmental protection and improved management of renewable natural resources. In both rural and urban Africa, the poor are affected the most by the loss of natural resources and environmental services. They are also at the greatest risk from natural disasters, particularly droughts and floods, whose impacts are aggravated by environmental degradation. The national economies of African countries also rely heavily on agriculture and on extraction of renewable natural resources for the income needed to provide the basic services and development essential for the poor.

Yet this natural resource base on which so much depends is steadily deteriorating, and the capacity of natural systems to produce goods and services is being lost. Africa has some of the world's highest rates of soil erosion and deforestation, as well as declining rangelands, wetlands, and fish and wildlife populations. Climate variation, already a serious threat to livelihoods and economic development in much of the region, is likely to be further aggravated by climate change within the next few decades. In Africa, better environmental management is not just about preserving nature or even about sustainable economic development: it is a matter of survival.

The Strategic and Regional Context

The Africa Region Environment Strategy (ARES) outlines the World Bank's commitment to help its clients achieve sustainable poverty reduction through better environmental management. It identifies the most urgent issues at the interface of environment and poverty and discusses targeted actions for addressing them. It reviews the lessons from experience to date and proposes new approaches. The strategic context in which the ARES has evolved and will be implemented is defined by the Bank's mission statement and operational policies, the World Bank Environment Strategy (WBES), and by the Bank's broader objectives, priorities, and strategies in the Africa Region.

1

Like the WBES, the ARES approaches environment through a "poverty lens" and targets four main objectives: (a) ensuring sustainable livelihoods, (b) improving environmental health, (c) reducing vulnerability to natural disasters, and (d) maintaining local, regional, and global ecosystems and values. Reflecting both the WBES's and the Bank's overall strategic objectives in Africa, key elements of the ARES include integrating environment into development and poverty reduction strategies; building an enabling environment and the institutional and human capacity for sustainable environmental management; promoting environmentally sustainable and equitable private sector–led economic development; improving governance in the public sector; encouraging decentralization and Community-Driven Development; and linking local and global environmental objectives. The ARES also takes into account the "real world" context of the opportunities and challenges of Africa today, such as the ecological, social, and political diversity of the region; the many urgent development priorities facing African countries; weak institutional capacity; and limited technical and managerial resources. It also recognizes the need for tradeoffs and compromises between short-term and longer-term objectives and among the interests of different stakeholders.

A healthy environment is essential to human welfare. At the same time, the constraints and avenues to improved environmental management mainly arise from human needs and actions. There is thus a strong linkage between environmental and social agendas, and tools such as stakeholder analysis, participatory processes, and community mobilization and capacity building are essential elements in improving environmental management. In the World Bank this linkage is reflected institutionally in the Africa Region Environment and Social Development Unit (AFTES).

Despite a widespread perception that the region is stagnating, many African countries have made significant progress in economic, social, and political development over the past few decades. But this progress is fragile and at risk owing to four urgent factors that threaten the region's prospects for growth and development: (a) rapid population growth, (b) political conflicts, (c) the HIV/AIDS (human immunodeficiency virus/acquired immunodeficiency syndrome) crisis, and (d) environmental degradation. The ARES aims to help African countries and people reverse environmental degradation in order to sustain and strengthen economic development, while recognizing that it cannot be achieved unless the other threats are also addressed.[1]

Urgent Issues at the Poverty-Environment Interface

Certain aspects of environmental degradation stand out as particularly urgent issues in Africa, by virtue of their prevalence, magnitude, and impacts on the poor. They are as follows:

SUSTAINABLE LIVELIHOODS. The majority of Africans live in rural areas and are poor. Given that they are dependent on renewable natural resources, the continuing decline of this resource base is the highest-priority environmental issue in Africa. The significance of land degradation and desertification, the deterioration and growing scarcity of surface water and groundwater, and the decline of such key natural resources as woodfuels and fish are well recognized. Less appreciated is the impact of the loss of productive natural ecosystems, whose intact value is often far greater than the sum of their component natural resource parts. Forests, wetlands, and rangelands are all being converted or degraded at a rapid rate across much of Africa, with catastrophic consequences for the poor, who are losing their livelihood base. Some of these losses are due to mismanagement, others to purposeful changes in land use. But the poor are rarely the main beneficiaries of these changes and are often left without alternatives or compensation. Thus, although it is conventional to speak of tradeoffs between conservation and economic development or poverty alleviation, in many cases the actual tradeoff may be between large-scale economic development and local impoverishment because natural ecosystems have not been conserved. At a national level, direct and immediate impacts of ecosystem destruction include flooding, siltation of dams, and loss of indigenous natural products such as medicinal plants, foods (including famine reserves), woodfuel, and building materials.

ENVIRONMENTAL HEALTH. Environmental health impacts are of great concern to African stakeholders. Poor health reduces peoples' survival rates and quality of life and affects their capacity to carry out economically and socially productive activity. Africans suffer a higher total burden of disease than do their counterparts in other regions. Environment, health, and poverty overlap extensively in Africa because many of the most widespread and debilitating diseases, particularly those that affect the poor disproportionately, stem from environmental conditions. This means that they may also be mitigated through improved environmental management (such as sanitation). This is usually more cost-effective than technical or clinical approaches aimed at repairing damage already done. Although it is not always recognized as an important issue in Africa, water and air pollution from domestic and industrial sources affects hundreds of millions of people in the region, particularly those living along marine and freshwater coastlines and in mining or industrial areas. African industrial establishments tend to be smaller than those in other parts of the world, but they are often poorly regulated and can have significant additive and cumulative impacts. Biomedical waste is also a growing hazard, given the lack of suitable incineration facilities at most hospitals and clinics. Ironically, efforts to stem the HIV/AIDS crisis are contributing to the problem through the upsurge in contaminated disposable syringes, needles, and condoms. The loss of natural ecosystems discussed above is also resulting in the loss of traditional medicines. In many African countries, up to 90 percent of the population uses traditional medicines, either by choice or because of lack of access to modern alternatives. Both the medicinal species and the associated indigenous knowledge are threatened by development that does not value them sufficiently.

SECURITY: VULNERABILITY TO NATURAL EVENTS AND DISASTERS. As a region, Africa is characterized by a high degree of climate variability, particularly in rainfall. This has chronic and severe impacts on livelihoods and economic development. Long (multiyear) dry periods and heavy rains that cause flooding are a recurring reality that must be systematically factored into development planning and assistance at all levels. As with health, prior protective ecological and risk management is likely to be more cost-effective than relief and reconstruction. The severity of natural disasters such as droughts and floods, which represent the extremes of climate variability, may be aggravated by environmental degradation. For example, both flooding and long dry spells become much more dangerous if the natural vegetation that helps hold moisture in the soil has been lost. The toll of such events on the livelihoods and security of the poor is immense. Poor people typically reside on marginal lands susceptible to floods and droughts, live in substandard housing, have less access to early warning systems and shelters, are more dependent on annual production from rainfed agriculture, and have limited economic resources to cope with catastrophic events.

THE GLOBAL ENVIRONMENT. In addition to being an essential resource for African peoples and economies, the region's vast and unique biodiversity endowment is an invaluable world heritage. This includes its remaining extensive natural habitats (including the Congo Basin forest, the second largest contiguous tropical rain forest area in the world), as well as wild relatives and "landraces" of important food and commercial crops and livestock. The direct cause of most biodiversity loss in Africa is conversion of natural habitats and water bodies to agriculture and other uses. Overexploitation for charcoal, commercial logging, and hunting for both local and international markets is also a significant threat in many cases. Landowners and resource users have little direct incentive to conserve biodiversity because the benefits of conservation are generally long term and diffuse, whereas the activities that destroy biodiversity often yield immediate individual benefits. Africa is not a large-scale user of fossil fuels compared with other regions.[2] The region's main contributions to global carbon emissions are from natural gas flaring from oilfields in a few countries, and from large-scale and ubiquitous burning of grasslands and forests. Africa may be the region most vulnerable to climate change, which is expected to cause even greater variability in rainfall and increases in average temperatures, particularly in the Sudan-Sahelian and southern subregions. Large, heavily populated areas that are now marginal could become uninhabitable or uncultivable through increased droughts, floods, or rising sea levels. This will further increase the already substantial number of "environmental refugees" and aggravate political conflicts. Again, it is the poor, dependent on rainfed agriculture and with tenuous land security, who will be most affected. Existing hydropower shortages are also likely to worsen, with negative impacts on production and growth, and there is evidence that vector-borne diseases such as malaria are spreading into new areas as a result of climate shifts.

Development Trends and Challenges

It is difficult to generalize across a region that is so ecologically, socially, economically, and politically diverse. However, a number of common development trends present challenges and opportunities for environmental management across the region. These include rapid and unplanned urbanization, the growing role of the private sector, decentralization and democratization, subregional integration, and globalization. Depending on how they are managed, these development trends could prove good or bad for Africa's environment and its future. Institutional and human resource capacities are key to influencing how all these development trends will affect environment and poverty. On the whole, Africa's institutions and populations are poorly equipped to deal with them and must be strengthened and empowered with these important challenges in mind.

Lessons from World Bank Experience

The Bank's environmental program over the past few decades has included direct investment in environmental improvements and indirect interventions aimed at creating capacity and an enabling environment for better environmental management. The experience gained from these efforts has been mixed, providing some promising models and pilot initiatives and important lessons for a forward-looking strategy.

The Environmental Assessment (EA) process represents a potentially powerful instrument for ensuring that environmental issues are identified and addressed, at least from a "do-no-harm" perspective. Substantial environmental investments can also originate from the Environment

Management Plans (EMPs) that are a product of the EA process. However, EA as currently used has significant limitations: it is generally project specific, often introduced too late in the project cycle to influence design, and more useful for mitigating negative impacts than for stimulating positive environmental action. Furthermore, the Bank's operational lending portfolio is evolving, with greater emphasis on instruments such as sectoral programs, budget support (Poverty Reduction Strategy Credit [PRSC], Public Expenditure Review Credit [PERC]), Community-Driven Development (CDD), and Social Funds. Methods for applying EA in these contexts are not well developed, although there are some guidelines and examples of Strategic or Sectoral Environmental Assessment (SEA) to draw upon. Most significantly, clients within and outside the Bank still often regard EA, and the Bank's Safeguard Policies in general, as externally imposed "conditionality" and obstacles, rather than as a positive means to improve the quality and impact of operations. As a result, the execution of EMPs and impact monitoring during implementation are often poor. This highlights the need for building constituency and capacity in-country rather than simply ensuring compliance with the Bank's Safeguard Policies in Bank-financed operations.

In recent years the Global Environment Facility (GEF) has also been instrumental in introducing environmental elements into many Bank-financed programs and operations. Difficulties sometimes encountered include a lack of understanding of GEF objectives and processes and a lack of government support and stakeholder ownership for projects whose benefits are perceived to be mainly international rather than national and local. One response has been to broaden the interpretation of the GEF mandate to better encompass regional priorities. For example, fighting land degradation and desertification was once eligible for GEF funding only when linked with biodiversity conservation or climate change. It is now a legitimate GEF target in itself. Support for biodiversity conservation, which had strongly emphasized protected areas, is increasingly being approached through integrated ecosystem management. Along with this evolution there has been a deliberate effort to reduce the number of free-standing, globally targeted GEF projects, in favor of blending GEF, International Development Association (IDA), and other donors' resources to support programs that generate local, national, and global benefits. The most common are community-based land and natural resource management projects that also seek to promote biodiversity conservation and sometimes carbon storage.

Mainstreaming environment into the broader development agenda remains an important challenge. In recent years the main vehicle for channeling environmental support has been National Environmental

Action Plans (NEAPs). These were often followed up by Environmental Support Programs (ESPs), financed by the Bank and other donors, to support implementation of the actions identified in the NEAPs. Although most ESPs have aimed at strengthening dedicated environmental policies and institutions, they have also included elements to promote environmental sustainability in development across a broad range of sectors. Several environmentally related regional information networks have also grown out of the NEAP process. Reviews of these support efforts have provided important lessons that have been incorporated into the ARES. These include the need for longer time frames to support institutional development and environmental action; the need for institutional capacity building to take into account the changing roles of government, civil society, and the private sector; the risk of isolating the environmental agenda from broader development (and thus limiting its constituency) by establishing isolated environmental planning processes, programs, and funds; the challenge of institutionalizing environment within sectoral agencies (for example, the inadequacy of the one-person "Environment Focal Point" approach); and the risk of creating overly ambitious and ultimately ineffective institutions through short-term external funding at levels far above what governments and other stakeholders will be able to sustain. The ARES also draws upon the experience and lessons from a wide array of projects and programs (for example, community-based natural resource management, private sector development, agricultural development and intensification) financed by the Bank and others, which have incorporated environmental sustainability to varying degrees.

Priorities for Action

The priorities for action are organized under the ARES in several ways for different purposes.

The description of "thematic priorities" follows the model of the World Bank Environment Strategy (WBES), which defines the World Bank's overall objectives in environment as improving the quality of life, the quality of (economic) growth, and the quality of the global commons. Under "quality of life," the ARES addresses enhancement of natural resource–based livelihoods through sustainable management of soils, water, and biological resources; protecting peoples' health from environmental burdens, including pollution and environmentally related diseases; and reducing peoples' vulnerability to environmental risks and natural disasters. Under "quality of growth," the ARES emphasizes improved environmental "governance," decentralization and associated empowerment of rural communities, and strengthening of both regulatory and incentive frameworks to encourage environmentally sustainable private sector investment. Under "quality of the global commons," the priorities identified are promoting subregional and regional cooperation in management of shared environmental resources (particularly water and wildlife); strengthening African countries' capacity to predict and adapt to the impacts of climate change; and assisting African countries to participate in international efforts to achieve global environmental objectives and capture a substantial share of the emerging markets for global environmental services.

Second, the ARES recognizes that Africa's great ecological and social diversity means that priorities for action are different in different parts of the region. The section on subregional priorities divides the continent into six subregions characterized by similar environmental conditions and socioecological challenges, and consequently similar priorities for environmental action to alleviate poverty: the Sudano-Sahelian Belt, humid West Africa, the Congo Basin, East Africa, southern Africa, and the Indian Ocean Islands. The high-priority environmental management objectives for each subregion emphasize issues that affect the livelihoods, health, and security of the poor; opportunities for economic development based on environmental resources; and unique global assets under threat. Some issues, such as land degradation, are equally significant across the continent, whereas others, such as coastal zone management and water scarcity, are more localized.

While environment is intrinsically cross-sectoral, most governments, donor organizations, and development programs are organized along sectoral lines. Therefore, to a large extent environmental objectives will be achieved through actions within sectoral programs, that is, by making environmental soundness and sustainability integral objectives and recognized elements of their success. The ARES outlines sectoral priorities for Africa, that is, priority environmental issues and outcomes for a number of key sectors (in summary in table 4.1 and in greater detail in appendix A). Sectors targeted for their strong significance to environmental management include agriculture and rural development, natural resource management, energy, urban development, water resource management, transport, health, and private sector development.

The ARES also identifies three urgent cross-cutting priorities that provide the essential basis for all the above actions to succeed: (a) adopting "people-focused ecosystem management"as a core principle for sustainable development, (b) building an enabling environment for environmental management, and (c) mobilizing resources for environmental management.

Integrated Ecosystem Management (IEM) has become widely recognized as the cornerstone of the environmental agenda (World Resources

Institute 2000). Simply put, it means preserving natural ecological systems such as water, energy and nutrient cycles, species complexes, and food webs. This in turn maintains the capacity of ecosystems to function and produce the food, fiber, energy, and other environmental goods and services that are essential to life. Beyond IEM as an environmental agenda, the ARES identifies a "people-focused" ecosystem management approach to development as the key to meeting human needs and enhancing economic production on a sustainable basis. Adopting an IEM approach has important strategic and operational implications. For example, land and resource use must be planned and coordinated over large landscapes (often across political borders) and among many different stakeholders; compromises and tradeoffs must be made among different environmental and development objectives; and both up-to-date information on the status and trends of ecosystems and a clear understanding of the processes that sustain them are needed.

Environmental management is not something that can be done once and then ignored, nor can it be solely the responsibility of a few people or institutions. For a real and lasting impact, maintaining a healthy and productive environment must be everyone's goal and everyone's business. Therefore, the ARES's highest priority is to help its clients put in place a political, social, economic, and institutional environment that motivates and enables a wide range of people and institutions to manage and protect the environment based on their own recognized interests. The essential elements of such an enabling environment are a broad and informed consensus on environmental and sustainable development objectives; policy, regulatory/legal, and institutional frameworks to support these objectives; and participatory mechanisms to track results and feed them back into decisionmaking processes. Efforts to develop these elements in the region have had limited success to date. To achieve greater success in the future, we must focus on reversing the incentives that currently drive people, individually and collectively (institutions), to destroy and degrade the environment. At the same time we must provide the essential technical and institutional tools for better environmental stewardship. Technical tools include environmental information, knowledge management, economic analysis, and appropriate technology. Institutional tools go beyond the common concept of public and private sector organizations to encompass all aspects of the "rules of the game" that provide the means for translating intention and policy into collective action. To achieve better results than in the past, our support for institutional development must explicitly acknowledge and address significant "real world" constraints and obstacles such as vested interests and "turf" issues, the slow pace of change in institutional cultures, financial limitations, and political considerations.

These endeavors will inevitably require a substantial commitment of human and financial resources over a long period of time. Therefore, a key objective over the next 5 to 10 years will be to generate sustainable funding for environmental management. A large part of this funding must be achieved through "internalizing environmental externalities" in the form of user fees, taxes, and other economic and market-based instruments. There is also an urgent need to reduce aid dependency and increase the role of internal resources and private sector investment for environmental management and protection, as international aid is variable and finite and will never be adequate to meet the full scope of the needs. This includes developing and capturing a substantial share of emerging markets for local and global environmental services such as water supply and purification, biodiversity conservation, and carbon sequestration. African countries can also benefit from a worldwide trend toward increased corporate commitment to environmental stewardship and social equity, but they must be vigilant so that they do not become a "dumping ground" for corporations seeking to escape this trend.

There is a close correlation between the priorities for action identified in the ARES and those identified by African leaders in the Environment Initiative of the New Partnership for African Development (NEPAD). For example, soil and water management (combating desertification), wetland conservation, coastal management, cross-border conservation, and adaptation to climate change are all highlighted in both the ARES and NEPAD. Similarly, the ARES's cross-cutting priority of creating an enabling environment for environmental management covers the same policy, institutional, and capacity issues as the NEPAD's proposed Environmental Governance Initiative.

Implementation of the Strategy

The ARES, together with several associated strategies (for example, the Joint Operational Strategy for Biodiversity Conservation and Forest Management, the Integrated Coastal Zone Management Strategy, and the GEF Strategy), will serve as a guiding framework for the World Bank's Africa Region, over the next five years, to achieve three objectives:

- Further enhance the environmental quality of the Bank's lending operations, including both project-based and nonproject lending
- Build an enabling environment and strengthen environmental management capacity within the region at all levels
- Mainstream environment in economic development at policy and operational levels.

Specific activities within this framework include the following:

- Improving the application of EA and other environmental and social Safeguard Policies both in project preparation and implementation and by influencing policies and planning through Strategic Environmental Assessment (SEA)
- Reorienting Environmental Support Programs (ESPs), from an emphasis on dedicated environmental institutions and initiatives to building a broad base of multisectoral environmental management capacity, and to strengthen both regulatory and incentive-based instruments
- Moving toward longer-term programmatic operations that combine concrete, substantive goals for improving environmental quality with a flexible, "adaptive management" approach to implementation
- Developing and supporting the information base and analysis needed for mainstreaming environment and making rational tradeoffs between competing objectives and interests
- Developing meaningful and practical indicators for assessing environmental conditions and trends, environmentally related poverty impacts, and the degree of integration of environment in development planning and operations
- Introducing an ecosystem and landscape-based approach to natural resource management and area development initiatives, including those that transcend national borders.

Given the broad scope of the environmental agenda and the large number of countries in the region, the Bank must be selective about the types of interventions it undertakes and the countries where it concentrates its efforts and resources. Building on the Bank's comparative advantage, the emphasis will be on establishing an enabling environment at the policy level, both through technical assistance and dialogue and through linkage with large-scale budget support and sectoral investment programs. Individual investment operations will increasingly be in the context of multisectoral and multidonor umbrellas such as the PRSC's Comprehensive Development Framework. For mainstreaming at the macroeconomic and policy levels, priority will be given to countries with clear environmental-poverty linkages and a willingness on the part of both the government and the Bank country team to support environmental analysis and consultation processes and incorporate their outputs. Other considerations include a strong ongoing dialogue and a substantial and diverse Bank lending program, providing leverage and opportunities for engagement and action across a range of sectors and programs. For mainstreaming at an operational level, priority criteria will include opportunities to contribute to the development of sectoral strategies with strong environmental-poverty linkages, situations in which the policy framework empowers local stakeholders, and situations in which ongoing or prospective development presents an urgent threat to locally or globally significant environmental assets.

Financial and technical resources for implementing the ARES are expected to come from (a) country programs for country-specific economic and sector work (ESW) and operations; (b) an "off the top" allocation and a regional "tax" on task budgets for strengthening the application of environmental and social Safeguard Policies; (c) regional budget allocations for implementation of the ARES and associated environmental strategies that enhance the understanding and application of environmental and social Safeguard Policies, as well as for studies and other activities with wider application such as development and piloting of methodologies and tools; (d) Bank-wide instruments such as the Mainstreaming Fund for Environment, Institutional Development Facility, Research Grants, and national and multinational Trust Funds; and (e) financial and in-kind support in the context of strategic partnerships.

Strategic partnerships will be vital to the implementation of the ARES, as its challenges transcend the Bank's own capacity. In addition to traditional partners such as bilateral donors and international and local nongovernmental organizations (NGOs), the Bank will continue to explore collaborations with the private sector in areas such as technology development and transfer, specialized training and information exchange, and environmental cleanup. Key criteria for developing and implementing these partnerships include ensuring that they address the countries' and the Bank's strategic priorities and are in the best interests of the client, that administrative costs are minimized but fully supported, and that they are totally in accordance with the Bank's Safeguard and fiduciary policies and obligations.

The ARES Implementation Matrix (appendix A) summarizes priorities and targets at a regional level for the next five years. Specific initiatives and resource requirements to meet these targets will be developed during the first year through consultation with senior management, country teams, and clients.

1
Introduction

Poverty and Environment in Africa

In Africa, perhaps more than in any other region, the World Bank's mission to fight poverty with lasting results is inescapably linked with environmental protection and improved management of renewable natural resources. In both rural and urban settings, the poor are affected the most by the loss of natural resources and the deterioration of environmental services. Their livelihoods depend heavily on rainfed agriculture and on natural systems to supply water, maintain soil fertility, and provide woodfuels and other essential products, and they have few alternatives or options to compensate when these are lost. Women are often affected more than men, as in many areas they are primarily responsible for cultivating food crops and obtaining water and fuel to support the household. As these resources decline, their task becomes increasingly difficult and time-consuming. The national economies of African countries also rely mainly on agriculture and on extraction of mineral and biological resources to generate the income needed to provide basic services and for development essential for the poor.

The natural resource base on which so much depends is steadily deteriorating. Soil degradation has affected 65 percent of Africa's cropland (the highest percentage in the world), and more than 20 million hectares of forest have been lost since 1980. Current annual rates of forest loss across the region average 0.7 percent (compared with 0.3 percent worldwide) and exceed 1 percent in at least 12 countries. One important impact of deforestation is the loss of indigenous medicinal plants, which represent the primary health care system for many millions of African people—it is estimated that 90 percent of people in West Africa use traditional medicines. Many coastal, marine, and freshwater fisheries that provide the main source of protein for much of the population are also threatened by overfishing and by reduced surface water flows and pollution. Overall, in Africa, as elsewhere in the world, the capacity of natural systems to produce the goods and services on which livelihoods

13

depend is declining, and it is the poor who suffer the most as a result. Worldwide too, the poor are affected the most by environmental health risks, and Africa leads the world in the proportion of disease burden arising from unclean water and poor sanitation, malaria, and (together with India) indoor air pollution.

At the same time, the poor of Africa are the people at the greatest risk worldwide from natural disasters, particularly droughts and floods.[3] Between 1965 and 1999, 770 natural disaster events of various scales have occurred in Africa, with an average frequency of 15 per country per year, killing more than 1.5 million people and affecting some 330 million others. The number of occurrences and their impacts are also increasing: the frequency has more than doubled in the last 15 years and the numbers of people killed and affected have doubled and tripled. Environmental degradation plays a significant role in aggravating the impacts of these events, particularly on the poor, who are the least able to avoid, escape, or cope with their effects.

These factors have momentous implications for the livelihoods, welfare, and economic development prospects of the people of the region today, and even more so for future generations if current trends are not halted and reversed. Improving the management of the environment is not just about preserving nature or even about sustainable economic development: ultimately, it is a matter of survival.

The Strategic and Regional Context

The Africa Region Environment Strategy (ARES) supports the World Bank's commitment to help its clients achieve sustainable poverty reduction through better environmental management. It identifies the most urgent issues at the interface of environment and poverty and outlines new approaches and targeted actions for addressing them based on current experience. The strategic context in which the ARES has evolved and will be implemented is defined by the Bank's mission statement and operational policies; the World Bank Environment Strategy (WBES); and the objectives, priorities, and strategies of the Bank's Africa Region Vice Presidential Unit (VPU). It is also defined by the priorities of African governments and other stakeholders, as articulated through regional organizations and initiatives (see box 1.1).

On an international level, the Millennium Development Goals (MDG) serve as a common, overarching target for sustainable development to which the Bank and many others are committed.[4] The Environment Goal calls for national strategies for sustainable development to be implemented in every country by 2005: "so as to ensure that current trends in the loss of environmental resources are effectively reversed at both

Box 1.1. Environmental Priorities of African Regional Organizations

Although most subregional and regional organizations in Africa were established to enhance economic development or political security, many have come to recognize the importance of environmental and natural resource management issues and have incorporated these objectives into their own objectives and programs.

Permanent Interstate Committee for Drought Control in the Sahel (CILSS). The committee was established in 1973 to support member states' efforts to combat drought and desertification. Initially focused on organizing and coordinating emergency food aid (1973–76), CILSS then shifted to promoting socioeconomic development, with an emphasis on farming, livestock, village water supply, and forestry. In 1985, it initiated a regional desertification control strategy, which led member states to draw up National Desertification Control Plans. The approach emphasizes integration of desertification control with land use planning. Subregional-level activities include gathering and sharing meteorological and hydrological data (Aghrymet Center); conducting research on drought resistance and on the interactions between resources, population, and environment (at the Sahel Institute); incorporating the environment into school curricula throughout the Sahel; and reforming natural resource–related policies and legislation in many countries.

Intergovernmental Authority on Drought and Development (IGADD). The authority was formed in 1986 with a relatively narrow mandate concerning issues of drought and desertification. During the 1990s IGADD became a vehicle for promoting regional security and political dialogue in the Horn of Africa. Its three priority areas for subregional cooperation are Conflict Prevention, Management and Resolution and Humanitarian Affairs; Infrastructure Development (transport and communications); and Food Security and Environmental Protection. Specific priorities include management of shared water resources (six transboundary lakes and rivers as well as contiguous coastal waters), deforestation, and land degradation and desertification.

Southern Africa Development Community (SADC). This organization was established in 1980 as the Southern African Development Coordination Conference and was reformulated as SADC in 1992. Article 5 of the SADC Treaty calls for sustainable utilization of natural resources and efficient protection of the environment.

The Environment and Land Management Sector was established in 1985, charged with helping member countries develop sustainable land management systems. SADC also has sector programs in Inland Fisheries,

(Box continues on the following page.)

Box 1.1. (continued)

Forestry, Wildlife, Marine Fisheries, and Tourism, among others. Water resource management is one of its major focal areas, including a legally binding Protocol on Shared Watercourse Systems (signed in 1995), which has established multinational River Basin Commissions and River Authorities or Boards as well as a monitoring unit.

African Ministerial Conference on Environment (AMCEN). The conference was established in 1985 and is the highest-level regional organization dedicated to environmental issues. AMCEN's structure includes four ecosystem-based committees (Deserts and Arid Lands, Lakes and Lake Basins, Forests and Woodlands, Seas and Island Ecosystems) and eight networks with regional coordinating units (Environmental Monitoring, Climatology, Soils and Fertilizer, Water Resources and Water Research, Energy and Renewable Energy Research, Environmental Education and Training, Biological Diversity and Plant Genetic Center, and Science and Technology). AMCEN coordinates environmental issues within the region at a political/diplomatic level, such as preparation of an African Common Position on the 2002 Earth Summit. Among its activities on the ground is a program of pilot projects (currently covering some 150 villages and 30 pastoral areas) aimed at helping people achieve self-sufficiency in food and energy through use of traditional skills.

New Partnership for African Development (NEPAD). The partnership is an initiative of African leaders, articulating their common vision and shared conviction that they have a duty to eradicate poverty, to place their countries on a path of sustainable growth and development, and to participate in the world economy and body politic on new terms. Its operational priorities are set out in the form of seven main initiatives, including the Environment Initiative. The specific environmental areas identified for focus under NEPAD are the following:

- Combating desertification (rehabilitating degraded land and addressing the factors leading to degradation)
- Wetland conservation (emphasizing achievement of social and ecological benefits from private sector development)
- Control of invasive alien species (emphasizing labor-intensive initiatives)
- Coastal management (protecting and utilizing coastal resources)
- Global warming (emphasizing monitoring and regulation of impacts of climate change, again emphasizing labor-intensive actions)
- Cross-border conservation areas (seeking to boost conservation and tourism and thus create jobs)
- Environmental governance (securing the institutional legal, planning, training, and capacity-building requirements that underpin all of the above)
- Financing (seeking a "carefully structured and fair system for financing").

global and national levels by 2015… [and for] the proportion of the population without access to an improved water source to be reduced by at least one half between 1990 and 2015." The discussion behind the Environment Goal recognizes that human development depends on the environment's providing a range of goods and services, and the clear if complex (two-way) linkages between environmental conditions and poverty. It also draws attention to the fact that the poorest people are the most vulnerable to shocks from environmental change and natural catastrophes, as well as to the effects of waterborne diseases and polluted air. Finally, it notes that the livelihoods of around 1 billion rural people are at risk because of desertification and land degradation and up to two-thirds of the world's population are likely to be affected by water scarcity. These goals and the understanding behind them are strongly echoed in the ARES.

The Bank's mission statement is "to fight poverty with passion and professionalism, to help people help themselves and their environment, with lasting results." The World Bank Environment Strategy looks at environment through a "poverty lens" and targets three pillars for focusing environmental management on alleviating poverty with lasting results: improving environmental health, ensuring sustainable livelihoods, and reducing vulnerability to natural disasters. Maintaining global ecosystems and life support systems (pillar four) is recognized as fundamental to each of these objectives. Key elements of the strategy include integrating environment into development and poverty reduction strategies and programs; putting in place the policy, institutional, and social conditions to promote environmentally sustainable and equitable private sector–led development; and linking local and global environmental objectives. Because a healthy environment is essential for human welfare, and because the constraints and avenues to improved environmental management mainly arise from human needs and actions, there is a strong linkage between environmental and social agendas. In the World Bank, they are brought together in the Africa Region Environment and Social Development Unit (AFTES).

The Bank's development priorities for Africa echo these core objectives. The Bank recognizes the vital importance of continuing and accelerating economic development as the route to alleviating poverty, but also that this economic development must be more equitable, and give more attention to environmental and social sustainability, than has often been the case in the past. In addition to promoting sound private sector growth, regional priorities include improving governance in the public sector, promoting decentralization and community empowerment, and helping African countries to stem and manage the impacts of the crippling HIV/AIDS crisis. Sectoral strategies with which the ARES interfaces (for example, rural development, energy, agricultural development, forest management, and private sector development) also focus on these aims and priorities.

Reflecting these strategic objectives and priorities, the Bank's ARES aims to assist its clients to do the following:

- Make the transition to sustainable economic development through improving environmental and natural resource management
- Empower communities and individuals to make a sustainable living based on the natural resource endowments of the region and to take responsibility for managing them
- Reduce the burden of diseases and poor health by improving the quality of the environment in which people live
- Reduce the vulnerability of people and economies of the region to natural disasters and severe climatic events
- Manage and conserve the unique biological diversity of the region for themselves, their future generations, and the world
- Establish an enabling environment and build the capacity to achieve these objectives and maintain them over the long term.

In doing so, the ARES takes into account certain essential realities:

- Africa is too diverse—ecologically, socially, and politically—for any one strategy or solution to be universally applicable (one size does not fit all).
- The environmental agenda must compete with many urgent priorities both within the Bank and among its clients (and is generally at a disadvantage because of the relatively long-term nature of its benefits).
- While environmental challenges and solutions are fundamentally cross-sectoral, both the Bank and its clients are structured and operate mainly along sectoral lines.
- Sometimes it is necessary to address the proximate causes of urgent problems while working toward longer-term solutions for underlying causes.
- Environmental resources, processes, and issues do not respect political boundaries.
- Development sometimes involves tradeoffs, resulting in relative winners and losers.

2

Urgent Issues and Trends: Environment through a Poverty Lens

Africa's Fragile Progress

Africa is sometimes perceived as stagnant or even regressing economically. In fact, however, after 20 years of decline, Africa's economies are growing again. Most countries have embarked on reform programs intended to regain macroeconomic balance, and there are signs that these programs have started to pay off in some countries, as the reforms have contributed to the resurgence of growth in the second half of the 1990s. This is shown in increased investment, rising incomes, and in some cases decreases in extreme poverty. In the typical African country, output growth rose to about 4.3 percent in 1994–98. Thirty-one countries saw growth rates over 3 percent, and 13 countries grew by more than 5 percent in 1998. Agricultural output grew at a rate of 3.7 percent per year in the median country, well above previous levels, and private investment has increased by almost 3 percent of gross domestic product (GDP) in recent years in politically and economically stable countries of the region.

Contrary to common perception, Africa has many well-managed economies, particularly in macroeconomic terms. The top third of African countries rate similarly to their counterparts in other regions in the annual "Country Policy and Institutional Assessment" ratings. These include some of the richest African countries, but also many poor ones. At the same time, the private sector is growing under the influence of more favorable policies, new leaders are emerging at all levels of society, and democratization trends in many countries are changing political power structures. The private sector, NGOs, community groups, women's associations, and farmers' organizations are all increasingly active. The press is also an important and positive force in public debate. For further information, see World Bank (2000a).

Nonetheless, Africa's progress is fragile and at risk because of four urgent threats to the region's prospects for growth and development: rapid population growth, the HIV/AIDS crisis, political conflicts, and environmental degradation.

Population Growth

While there has been some decline in population growth in recent years, and further modest declines are projected in some countries, Africa's average population growth rate of 2.8 percent remains the highest in the world. In some countries the rate is considerably higher (see table 2.1). Although fertility rates have begun to decline in a few African countries, overall Africa is the only region where the 6- to 11-year age group is still growing. In addition, unlike other regions where the ratio of dependents to working-age population has fallen to one-half, the age-dependency ratio in Africa has remained close to 1 (World Bank 2000a). The impact of these demographic trends on poverty and economic development is well known: for example, it has been estimated that the continent's GDP must increase at about 5 percent per year simply to prevent an increase in the number of absolute poor. Rapid rates of population growth reduce the relative availability of services such as education and health, undermining the ability of people to raise themselves out of poverty.

High population densities and growth rates are not necessarily a constraint to development, as can be seen from countries such as Singapore and the Netherlands. But in many African countries, rapid population growth is increasingly overwhelming their physical, economic, and social service capacity to provide for the needs of their people. The results are high unemployment; malnutrition; overcrowded and underserviced squatter settlements, classrooms, and clinics; and smallholder farms subdivided to the point that they are too small to support a household. Factors such as highly skewed land distribution and land tenure policies, as well as historically low investment in human resources, aggravate the problem and limit peoples' opportunities and options.

Population growth is an important crosscutting issue that affects all aspects of environmental management, from pressure on the natural resource base to waste management and health. It also increases vulnerability to climate variability, as people are increasingly forced to occupy risky areas such as floodplains and steep slopes. At current rates of population growth and natural resource degradation, it is estimated that the region will be able to grow only enough food to meet the needs of 40 to 50 percent of its population by 2025.

HIV/AIDS

Nearly 34 million people in the world are currently living with HIV/AIDS, one-third of whom are young people between the ages of 10 and 24. Nowhere has the impact of HIV/AIDS been more severe than in Sub-Saharan Africa, which now contains two-thirds of the world's

Table 2.1. Population Growth Rates of Some African Countries

Country	Total population (thousands) 1998	Total population (millions) 2015	Average annual growth rate (percent) 1980–98	Average annual growth rate (percent) 1998–2015
Fastest growing				
Angola	12.0		3.0	2.8
Benin	5.9		3.0	2.5
Botswana	1.6		3.0	0.9
Congo, Dem. Rep. of	48.2		3.2	2.9
Gabon	1.2		3.0	2.2
The Gambia	1.2		3.6	2.2
Ghana	18.5		3.0	2.2
Kenya	29.3		3.1	1.7
Malawi	10.5		3.0	2.2
Niger	10.1		3.3	3.0
Tanzania	32.1		3.0	2.0
Togo	4.5		3.0	2.0
Slowest growing				
Burundi	6.5		2.6	2.0
Guinea	7.1		2.6	2.0
Guinea-Bissau	1.2		2.1	1.8
Lesotho	2.1		2.4	1.6
Mauritius	1.2		1.0	0.9
Mozambique	16.9		1.9	2.0
Rwanda	8.1		2.5	2.2
Sierra Leone	4.9		2.3	1.9
South Africa	41.4		2.3	1.0
Sudan	28.3		2.3	2.1
Sub-Saharan Africa	627.1		2.8	2.2

Source: World Bank (2000g).

HIV/AIDS-affected population. More than 11 million Africans have already died, and another 22 million are living with HIV/AIDS. At the national level, the 21 countries with the highest prevalence of AIDS are in Africa. In Botswana and Zimbabwe, one in four adults is infected. At the individual level, the risk is almost incomprehensible. A child born in Zambia or Zimbabwe is more likely than not to die of AIDS. In many other African countries, the lifetime risk of dying of AIDS is greater than one in three. Given the scale of the epidemic in Africa, it is no longer just a public health problem, it is a development crisis.

Because it kills people in the prime of their lives, AIDS has had a devastating impact on development: it decimates the work force, destroys and impoverishes families, makes orphans of millions of children, and tears apart communities. The World Bank report *Intensifying Action Against HIV/AIDS in Africa* (World Bank 2000e) points out that the costs AIDS imposes force countries to make heartbreaking choices between today's and future lives, and between health and dozens of other vital investments for development, including the environment.

Political Conflicts

The high number of political conflicts in Africa is seriously compromising development progress, perpetuating poverty, and increasing suffering. Of the 27 major armed conflicts in the world in the last year, 11 were fought in Africa, and currently about 20 percent of Africans live in countries formally at war or severely disrupted by conflict. There are about 4 million transborder refugees and 16 million internally displaced persons. Large concentrations of these refugees are often forced to eke out a living for months or years in forest areas and marginal rangelands where the resource base is the poorest and most fragile. Even when they are able to cultivate food or it is provided by relief organizations, the need for woodfuel and other products and income drives people to decimate the only resources available to them.

Political conflicts have obvious environmental impacts, such as large-scale deforestation and erosion. They can also have more subtle impacts, as in recent years when the presence of large numbers of refugees in the mid-altitude forests in Rwanda and the Democratic Republic of Congo (DRC) drove the endangered endemic mountain gorillas to unaccustomed higher elevations, where they suffered from respiratory diseases. Armed forces on all sides of the conflicts also deplete the areas' natural resources for sustenance or money to buy weapons and supplies. At the same time, resource scarcity and environmental stress are increasingly implicated in triggering or prolonging conflicts. In addition to identifying and alleviating potential environmental flash points through conflict management, postconflict environmental rehabilitation is essential for restoring livelihoods and can also help reduce the likelihood of a recurrence of hostilities. The Bank and other donors need to develop strategies to assist countries in both aspects.

Environmental Degradation

Environmental degradation is the fourth grave threat to Africa's prospects for economic growth and development. It undermines the fabric of national economies and individual livelihoods, from the loss of electrical generating power caused by siltation of dams, to desertification of formerly productive agricultural lands, to the displacement of tens of thousands of farmers and pastoralists when rivers dry up because of the destruction of their watersheds, to the collapse of vital fisheries. At a more subtle level, it reduces peoples' productivity both through illness and through loss of time spent gathering water and fuel.

The ARES aims to help countries and people in Africa reduce and reverse environmental degradation in order to sustain economic growth and development. It does not offer strategies for addressing the other three urgent threats to Africa's growth prospects, as they are the subject of other regional strategies, but we recognize that its objectives cannot be achieved unless these other factors are also addressed. Therefore, it is in the context of the added pressures caused by explosive population growth, the devastating AIDS epidemic, and the political conflict throughout the African continent that we must view and understand the environmental issues that confront Africa today.

Urgent Issues at the Poverty-Environment Interface

Within the framework of the four "pillars" of the poverty-environment interface, a number of aspects of environmental degradation stand out as urgent issues by virtue of their prevalence, magnitude, and impacts on the poor. The emerging issue of climate change is also expected to aggravate, amplify, and intensify the impacts of all these issues over the next several decades.

Threats to Sustainable Livelihoods

Given the predominance of the rural poor and the increasingly precarious nature of rural livelihoods in much of the region, degradation of the underlying natural resource base—land, water, and biological resources—is widely recognized as the highest-priority aspect of environmental degradation in Africa. Less recognized but equally significant is the loss of productive natural ecosystems, whose intact value is often far greater than the sum of their component natural resource parts.

LAND DEGRADATION AND DESERTIFICATION. Africa is a large continent, but only about 20 percent of its total land area is arable. Most of the remainder is either too steep for cultivation or too dry for rainfed agriculture and too far from water sources for economically viable irrigation (or it is already damaged through salinization from past irrigation). The average amount of land per capita is among the lowest in the world, ranging from about 0.1 to 0.6 hectare per capita. With more than 70 percent of the population made up of (mostly small-scale) agriculturalists, arable land is the single most vital natural resource of the region. Although there are some very fertile areas, much of Africa's soil is of relatively poor quality because of the continent's geological history and climate. Some soils are deficient in key nutrients (for example, phosphorus), have poor water retention, and are easily eroded and degraded. A global assessment of soil degradation (Oldeman 1990) as well as a World Bank strategy for development (World Bank 1996) indicated that across Africa, 65 percent of arable cropland and more than 30 percent of all permanent pasture are significantly degraded. Much of the erosion is due to cultivation on steep slopes and in marginally arable lands, using inappropriate farming practices. Traditional methods for restoring fertility are undermined by the growing land scarcity. In the Sudano-Sahelian Belt, rotation cycles of at least 5 to 6 years are needed to restore soil fertility through natural processes, but in practice about half of the arable land is under cultivation each year. High-yielding crop varieties, which have boosted production in other regions, are poorly suited for the low-input, rainfed agriculture that characterizes most of African food production that provides the livelihoods of the majority of the region's poor.

SCARCITY AND DETERIORATION OF SURFACE WATER AND GROUNDWATER. Fresh water, which is essential to life and livelihoods, is one of Africa's scarcest commodities. Much of Africa is regarded as "drought prone" because of the regular occurrence of successive dry years, leading to crop failures and famine. Protecting surface water and groundwater resources should be among the highest priorities of governments and individuals, but in most of the region water policies and use practices fail to reflect this.[5] Freshwater supplies are being rapidly depleted through inefficient use and polluted by industrial and domestic effluents. While domestic, industrial, energy generation, agricultural, and ecological uses of fresh water are all important, in many cases tradeoffs and choices have to be made among them. At present, water use decisions are often made without adequate information or process, with an influential minority often receiving a disproportionate share of the benefits.

LOSS OF PRODUCTIVE NATURAL ECOSYSTEMS. While most governments and people are familiar with the issues of land and water degradation, far fewer appreciate the significance of the loss of productive natural ecosystems. Forests, wetlands, and rangelands are all being lost or degraded at a rapid rate across much of Africa, with major consequences for the poor. The highest rates of forest loss are in areas with dense or rapidly growing populations, such as the East African Highlands and the Sahel. The primary cause of forest loss continent-wide is conversion of the land for agriculture, with exploitation for fuel wood and timber also a major factor in some areas. Woodfuels account for 70 percent of total energy use and 90 percent of household energy use in Africa, since they are the predominant fuel in urban as well as rural settings. One negative economic and livelihood impact of loss of forest ecosystems is deterioration of watersheds, resulting in droughts and flooding: of the region's 11 major multinational watersheds, 7 have lost more than 90 percent of their original forest cover and 4 have lost more than 99 percent (see table 2.2). Another serious impact is the deepening fuel wood shortage. If current trends continue, all countries in the Sudano-Sahelian Belt are expected to experience a severe woodfuel crisis by 2025.

Wetlands are the ecosystem type most rapidly being lost and degraded worldwide. Causes include excessive abstraction of water upstream, deliberate draining of swamps and marshes for cultivation, disruption of natural flooding cycles through damming and flood control works, and pollution from agricultural runoff and industrial and domestic effluents. Coastal wetlands, which are essential for sustaining stocks of fish and shellfish, are particularly threatened by pollution because of the rapid, unplanned, and inadequately serviced growth of coastal cities and large-scale tourism development. The negative impacts include loss of income and poor nutrition for the large numbers of fishing communities across

Table 2.2. Major African Watersheds

Watershed	Estimated area (km²)	Countries involved (number)	Population density (per km²)	Original forest lost (percent)
Chari	549	5	11.0	99.9
Congo	3,807	9	14.5	45.9
Juba-Shibeli	834	3	18.7	76.5
Limpopo	421	4	35.1	99.0
Niger	2,262	10	31.2	95.9
Nile	3,255	11	42.7	92.1
Okavango	721	4	2.6	0.2
Orange	941	4	12.3	99.9
Senegal	420	4	11.8	99.9
Volta	407	6	42.2	96.6
Zambezi	1,332	8	17.7	43.1

Source: World Resources Institute (1999).

the region, an increase in waterborne diseases, the loss of large areas of critical dry season grazing land for livestock and wildlife, and a decline in many resident and migratory bird species.

Rangelands across Africa are also declining because of overgrazing and agricultural expansion. The traditional pastoralist strategy for using fragile, semi-arid rangelands is to move herds regularly to allow grazed areas to recover. Certain areas are traditionally set aside as drought reserves. But agricultural expansion and other factors are interrupting these movements and undermining this strategy because pastoralists typically lack formal ownership or exclusionary rights over the land they use. This trend continues despite the fact that the agriculture that displaces rangelands is often inefficient or unsustainable, requiring high levels of public or private subsidy to survive. Government policies and economic trends generally promote settlement over nomadic or transhumant lifestyles, whereas climatic and political events often block traditional trek routes or cause people to concentrate around aid stations. Expansion of agriculture and the "squeezing" of pastoralists also heighten human/wildlife conflict, as people continue to move into the remaining wildlife areas, with the resultant competition for grazing land and water, crop and livestock raiding, and sometimes injury and loss of human life. In some cases, particularly in the eastern and southern African rangelands, agricultural expansion and other activities threaten a lucrative wildlife-based tourism industry.

It is conventional to speak of tradeoffs between conservation and economic development and poverty alleviation. In many cases, however, the actual tradeoff may be between large-scale economic development and local impoverishment because of a failure to conserve natural ecosystems. The rural poor are the most adversely affected by the loss of these natural ecosystems because they are the most directly dependent on them for both day-to-day livelihood and income. Perhaps the best-known example is the disastrous impact on local fishing communities of the establishment of a lucrative commercial exotic fishery in Lake Victoria (see box 2.1). There are also numerous examples of conversions of large areas of natural forest to commercial crops (for example, for cocoa production in Ghana and Côte d'Ivoire), displacing and impoverishing rural communities while increasing GNP at the national level.

The loss of biodiversity resources that usually accompanies the decline of natural ecosystems robs rural communities of many important assets, including medicinal plants, wild foods (including famine reserves), building and craft materials, and the like. For example, recent surveys conducted in a typical rural county in Zimbabwe found that on average each family derived more than 35 percent of its income from

---

Box 2.1. Lake Victoria Fisheries: A Cautionary Tale

Africa's Lake Victoria provides an example of how profound and unpredictable tradeoffs can be when management decisions are made without regard to how the ecosystem will react. Lake Victoria, bounded by Uganda, Tanzania, and Kenya, is the world's largest tropical lake. Its fish are an important source of food and employment for the subregion's 30 million people. Before 1970, Lake Victoria was home to more than 350 species of fish from the cichlid family, 90 percent of which were endemic. Today, more than half of those species are either extinct or found only in very small populations.

What caused such a profound collapse? In the 1950s overfishing had depleted the native species, and land use changes in the watershed dumped pollution and silt into the lake, increasing the nutrient load and causing lethal algal blooms. At that time two exotic fish species, the Nile perch and Nile tilapia, were introduced to the lake. The result was dramatic: by 1983, Nile perch made up almost 70 percent of the catch, with Nile tilapia and a native sardine making up most of the balance. While the introduced fish devastated the lake's biodiversity, they were a boon for the commercial fishery: today the Nile perch produces some 300,000 metric tons of fish, earning $280 million to $400 million in the export market. (All dollar amounts are U.S. dollars.) Ironically, the fishery does not benefit the local communities because they cannot afford the expensive equipment, such as heavy-duty nets and processing facilities, needed for the fishery. Even as Lake Victoria perch and tilapia grace the plates of diners as far away as Israel and Europe, the availability of fish has declined locally and protein malnutrition is now evident among the people of the lake basin. Even the long-term sustainability of the profitable Nile fish fishery is in doubt. Whereas the original lake species, the cichlids, could be air dried, the Nile species need firewood, putting additional pressure on the area's limited forests.

What in the 1950s appeared to be a logical approach to increasing the commercial potential of the ecosystem has in the 1990s turned into an environmental nightmare—long-term environmental sustainability was traded for a short-term profit. In the process, both the people of the lake and the rich ecosystem of Lake Victoria lost out.

---

forest products. Wild foods and other resources also serve as a safety net, permitting people to survive when crops fail or livestock perish. There may also be a significant opportunity cost, as some of the biodiversity that is lost could have great economic potential, either as tourism attractions or as medicinal or other products (see box 2.2 on *Prunus africanus*).

Box 2.2. Harvesting of *Prunus africanus*

The bark of an endemic African tree, *Prunus africanus*, is the source of pygeum, a widely used treatment for prostate disorders. The current annual international market for pygeum products is about US$220 million. One large tree can yield up to a metric ton of bark, worth about US$200. Most of the current supply comes from Cameroon (2,000 tons per year) and Madagascar (600 tons per year), although the species is found and exploited in a number of other countries as well.

  P. africanus grows in Afro-montane habitats between 900 and 3,400 meters, takes 15 to 20 years to produce seeds, and requires 12 to 15 years to produce bark, which contains the prostate remedy's active ingredient. The species is listed under Appendix II of the Convention on the International Trade in Endangered Species (CITES), where international trade is allowed with a CITES permit.

  Sustainable harvesting of the bark is possible by removing only strips from opposite sides of the trunk and allowing eight for regeneration before harvesting the adjacent panels. But much of the current harvest is destructive because it involves either stripping the entire tree or cutting it down. The species is also threatened by habitat destruction. A number of research institutes (for example, International Centre for Research in Agroforestry, the Kenya Forest Research Institute and the Cameroon Institut de Recherche Agronomique et Developpement) are collecting seeds from the remaining stands of wild trees and developing methods for artificial cultivation.

Source: Consultative Group on International Agricultural Research (2000).

Threats to Health

Health impacts are generally the highest priority environmental concern among African stakeholders. Poor health both reduces peoples' survival rates and quality of life and affects their capacity to carry out economically and socially productive activity. Africans suffer a higher total burden of disease than their counterparts in other regions. For example, illness is estimated to cause a loss of 6.5 percent of earnings per working adult in some African countries. Environment, health, and poverty overlap extensively in Africa because many of the most widespread and debilitating diseases, particularly those that affect the poor disproportionately, stem from environmental conditions. Therefore, they may also be mitigated through improved environmental management.

  The issue of environmental health has several dimensions. These range from environmentally related deseases to pollution and hazardous waste to the loss of traditional medicine.

ENVIRONMENTALLY RELATED DISEASE. As shown in table 2.3, three of the top five sources of morbidity and mortality in Africa (malaria, respiratory infections, and diarrheal diseases) are conditions that can be substantially ameliorated through environmental interventions such as the protection and purification of water supplies, sanitation and waste collection, and better indoor ventilation. For example, indoor air pollution from wood fires is the greatest cause of respiratory disease in Africa.

The 1993 *World Development Report: Investing in Health* (World Bank 1993) estimated that worldwide the public health care system could relieve about 33 percent of the burden of disease. By comparison, it has been estimated that in Sub-Saharan Africa, investment in health-related infrastructure could target up to 44 percent of the disease burden. Ongoing research indicates that measures inside and outside the health care system (for example, clinical interventions vs. sanitation infrastructure, cleaner cooking fuels, and the like) can each achieve about a 25 percent reduction in the overall disease burden. With public health services in Sub-Saharan Africa increasingly consumed by the growing HIV/AIDS crisis, alternative (cross-sectoral) measures for reducing other conditions are particularly important. Environmentally related interventions are also often more cost-effective than clinical approaches, because the same action, such as improving sanitation infrastructure or drainage in urban areas, can alleviate a number of health problems. They can also have other benefits, such as enhancing tourism revenues by reducing ambient health risks that may dissuade tourists from visiting.

Table 2.3. Rank and Share of the Burden of Disease in Sub-Saharan Africa, 1990 and 1998

Disease	1990 (percent)	1998 (percent)
HIV/AIDS and other sexually transmitted diseases	2.8	16.6
Malaria	9.2	10.6
Diarrheal diseases	10.9	7.5
Acute lower respiratory infections	10.2	7.0
Perinatal conditions[a]	6.5	6.2
Top five subtotal	39.6	47.9

a. "Childhood cluster" consisting of whooping cough, poliomyelitis, diphtheria, measles, and tetanus.
Sources: For 1990 figures, see Murray and Lopez (1996); for 1998 figures, see World Health Organization (1999).

POLLUTION. Pollution is not generally recognized as an important issue in Africa because a large proportion of the population is rural and there is a relatively low level of industrialization. Nevertheless, it is a problem that affects hundreds of millions of people, particularly those living along marine and freshwater coastlines and in mining areas. Many of Africa's coastal waters are heavily polluted by domestic and industrial wastes (particularly agroindustrial, fish processing, leather tanning, fabric dying, and the like), by the runoff of agrochemicals used for intensive commercial crops and livestock dipping, and by oil spills and chronic oil leakage. Although African industrial establishments tend to be smaller than in other parts of the world, they are often poorly regulated and can have significant additive and cumulative impacts. In addition to direct health impacts and destruction of fish and shellfish, coastal pollution can threaten tourism, which is often a major source of income and employment in the area. Serious air pollution is still limited to a few major cities (such as Lagos and Johannesburg), but it is increasing as the cities—and the number of motor vehicles in them—steadily grow.

HAZARDOUS WASTE. As with pollution in general, hazardous waste is a localized problem in Africa and is aggravated by a lack of capacity to handle and regulate it. There are infamous examples of companies from industrial nations "dumping" toxic wastes in Africa (either secretly or in collusion with mendacious leaders). One growing problem is biomedical waste because most hospitals and clinics lack suitable incineration facilities. Ironically, efforts to stem the HIV/AIDS crisis are contributing significantly to the problem, as the health infrastructure is not prepared to deal with the substantial increase in contaminated disposable syringes, needles, and condoms.

LOSS OF TRADITIONAL MEDICINES. Traditional healing is a major element in the health care of the majority of rural Africans, either because of cultural preference or because of their limited access to modern treatment facilities or drugs. In many countries it is estimated that up to 90 percent of the population uses traditional medicines. A wide variety of indigenous plant (and other) species are used in traditional medicine, many clearly demonstrated to contain effective active ingredients. Some, such as the Rosy Periwinkle of Madagascar, have been extracted and developed as important modern medicines. While the medicinal use of indigenous species is important in conferring value on biodiversity and natural ecosystems, there is a risk of overexploitation for local use or commercial trade (see box 2.2). Although this represents an important threat to some species, overall the greater threat is rapid rates of deforestation across the region.

Threats to Security: Vulnerability to Natural Events and Disasters

CLIMATE VARIABILITY. Africa experiences a high degree of climate variability, which has severe and chronic impacts on livelihoods and economic development. Long (multiyear) dry periods and heavy rains that cause rivers to overflow their banks are frequently occurring phenomena in Africa. They are a reflection of the extreme natural variability of rainfall in the region's extensive arid and semi-arid lands (ASAL), and the result of the complexities of its river basin system (see figure 2.1, which shows the variation in annual rainfall in Zimbabwe from 1980 to 1993). As such, they are a reality that must be systematically factored into development planning and assistance at all levels, with an emphasis on ecological and risk management rather than relief and reconstruction. Most important, we must recognize that although the reality of climate variability cannot be changed, its impact on the poor can be mitigated through environmental risk management. In many cases the traditional methods of environmental management, such as pastoralists' moving herds over large distances in search of grass and water, are no longer viable because of such factors as population growth and the spread of agriculture and settlements. We must help them to find and implement new methods that function in the context of current realities.

NATURAL DISASTERS AND EXTREME ENVIRONMENTAL EVENTS. Africa experiences a number of natural disasters and extreme environmental events, which are defined as droughts, floods, insect infestations, earthquakes, wildfires, wind-related phenomena, landslides, and erupting volcanoes. Some natural disasters, such as droughts and floods, represent the extremes of climate variability. Others, such as landslides and wildfires, can be triggered or aggravated by environmental degradation. In either case, their toll on the livelihoods and security of the poor is immense. According to the *World Disasters Report* (International Federation of Red Cross and Red Crescent Societies 1993), the citizens of low-income countries are on average at three to four times greater risk of dying in a disaster than those in high-income countries. Poor people typically reside on marginal lands susceptible to floods, droughts, and the like; live in substandard housing; have less access to early warning systems and shelters; are more dependent on annual production of rainfed agriculture; and have limited economic resources to cope with catastrophic events.

The poor of Sub-Saharan Africa are particularly vulnerable to droughts and floods. There were an estimated 330 droughts in the region between 1965 and 1999 (a rate of 17 per year), with the largest number

Figure 2.1. Annual Mean Rainfall in Zimbabwe, 1980–1995

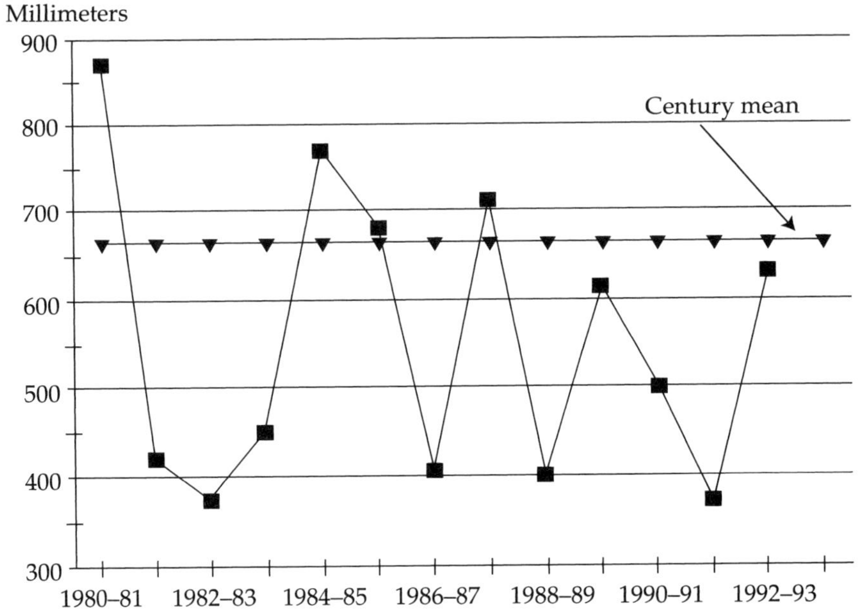

Millimeters

Source: Data are from the Climate Prediction Center of the U.S. National Oceanic and Atmospheric Agency and were obtained from the International Research Institute for Climate Prediction (Palisades, N.Y.). See also Janowiak and Xie (1999).

(11) in Sudan. The peak drought years were 1982, 1983, 1984, and 1992. The number of deaths attributed to drought during that period, 880,787, is 84 times higher than those related to floods, which represent the second-most-deadly natural disaster. During the peak flood years of 1989, 1990, 1998, 1999, and 2000, major floods occurred in Burkina Faso, Chad, Kenya, Madagascar, Mozambique, Nigeria, Sudan, and Zimbabwe. Natural disasters represent extremes of climate variation (droughts, floods), often with scale and impacts aggravated by environmental degradation. For example, typically long dry spells become much more dangerous if natural vegetation has been lost, leaving nothing to protect the topsoil from wind erosion.

Ethiopia is by far the Sub-Saharan African country most vulnerable to natural disasters, particularly droughts and insect infestations, both of which have a strong impact on famine and therefore on the poor. Other countries experiencing high occurrences and impacts of natural disasters are Madagascar, Mozambique, South Africa, Sudan, and Tanzania, followed by Benin, Burkina Faso, Chad, Kenya, Malawi, Mali, Mauritania, Niger, Senegal, and Uganda (World Bank 2000f).

Threats to the Global Environment

Africa is very significant from a global environmental perspective. In addition to being an essential resource for African peoples and economies, the region's vast and unique biodiversity endowment is an invaluable world heritage. This includes not only the biodiversity in its remaining natural habitats (including the Congo Basin forest, the second largest continuous tropical rainforest area in the world), but also wild relatives and "landraces" of important food and commercial crops and livestock. These species and varieties, which often have valuable traits such as disease resistance or adaptation to extreme climates, represent an irreplaceable source of genetic material for breeding programs worldwide. Africa's forests and rangelands also represent an enormous reservoir of carbon in their biomass and soil that, if released through burning or other destructive practices, can contribute substantially to the concentration of atmospheric carbon (greenhouse gases). An estimated 20 percent of worldwide annual anthropogenic carbon emissions arise from tropical deforestation. The international community provides considerable support to address these global concerns. The challenge, however, is to assist African countries to capture a greater share of these resources and to use in capturing them in ways that provide both local and global benefits.

BIODIVERSITY LOSS. The single greatest source of biodiversity loss in Africa and worldwide is conversion of natural habitats to agriculture and other uses. Enormous expanses of forest and savanna lands have been cleared for commercial cultivation, much of it low yielding and unsustainable and sometimes abandoned after only a few years. In arid and semi-arid areas, great expanses of rangeland can become unusable for wildlife (and for pastoralists) when the scarce surface water sources are appropriated for irrigation. Commercial logging is a serious threat not only because forest habitats are directly destroyed but also because logging roads provide access to agriculturalists. In some areas, such as the lowland forests of West Africa and the Congo Basin, hunting is a major threat because of the enormous and virtually insatiable market for "bushmeat" in both rural and urban areas and the lax enforcement of wildlife protection laws. These are the proximate causes of biodiversity loss. It is conventional to say that the ultimate cause is poverty (sometimes coupled with human population growth). However, the same factors are not driving domestic species of animals and plants into extinction. The important difference lies in the fact that domestic crops and livestock generally belong to individuals, whereas most wild biodiversity is usually regarded and treated as a common property (effectively an open access) resource. The benefits that local communities and individuals derive from indigenous biological resources (while often considerable) are less than those they derive from land uses that displace and destroy biodiversity. Therefore, individuals, corporations, and governments all generally have greater incentives to exploit biological resources for short-term gain than to preserve them for the long term. Stemming and reversing the trends of biodiversity loss require addressing these ultimate causes, rather than only trying to change the proximate behavior.

CLIMATE CHANGE. With many urgent, immediate environmental issues vying with economic and social issues for attention and resources, long-term threats such as climate change tend to be overlooked or deferred. But that would be a serious mistake for Africa. The region, which already labors under a heavy burden of natural disasters because of climate variability, will be particularly vulnerable to the impacts predicted by some models of climate change. Its effect will be to aggravate and increase all the environmental issues discussed above.

For example, certain parts of Africa are predicted to be among the most severely affected areas of the world in terms of physical effects, such as increased variability of rainfall and the incidence and severity of climatic events such as cyclones, droughts, and floods. Overall, the Horn of Africa region is expected to be affected the most by reduced precipitation, but drier conditions are also expected in parts of the Sahel and southern Africa. Average precipitation is expected to increase only in the already moist areas of western Africa.

Aside from the obvious agricultural and health impacts, reduced and unpredictable rainfall has a major economic impact through power shortages in the many African countries that rely heavily on hydropower for industrial and domestic energy. Power rationing and load shedding resulting from depleted reservoirs have already adversely affected the economies of a number of African countries in recent years. Climate change is also expected to lead to sea level rise, which would affect the large populations living in coastal and low-lying delta areas, along with substantial infrastructure investments. North Africa and the Sahel are expected to experience the greatest increases in average temperature, which will shift and in some cases reduce growing seasons and arable regions. Higher temperatures will also lead to increased evaporation (estimates up to 10 percent in northern Africa) and therefore reduced availability of surface water. There is also evidence that increased temperatures are associated with the spread of some vector-borne diseases, such as malaria, which is already being reported at elevations where it was previously unknown.

African countries and the rural poor are especially vulnerable to such changes both because they depend on agriculture and because they generally lack the financial, technical, and institutional resources to adapt to and cope with the impacts. The widespread reliance on rainfed agriculture, together with the growing scarcity of arable land and the trend toward cultivation in increasingly marginal areas, means that even relatively small changes in average temperature, precipitation, and water balance are likely to have very serious implications. These impacts will disproportionately affect the poor, who generally occupy the most marginal agricultural lands and lack the resources to invest in ameliorative measures such as irrigating the land, digging deeper wells, and shifting to alternative varieties or crops. At the national level, the greatest impact on GDP may be expected in western Africa because of the economic importance of export-oriented commercial agriculture.

In addition to the direct impacts on livelihoods and health, increased environmental stress resulting from climate change may be expected to increase the already substantial problem of "environmental refugees," aggravating political conflicts and further straining weak government budgets.

On the other side of the equation, many African countries and landholders would do well to position themselves to participate in the emerging international market in "carbon offset credits," which is already a reality in the private sector and recently received a substantial boost under the Kyoto Protocol of the Climate Change Convention. Through the "Clean Development Mechanism" under the Convention, industrial nations can meet some of their obligation to reduce greenhouse gas emissions by "buying" the rights to tons of carbon that are either removed from the atmosphere or actively prevented from entering the atmosphere through actions taken in developing countries. The most common application of this concept has been investments to reduce carbon emissions from industrial processes and energy generation. With the exception of Nigeria and South Africa, African countries have little comparative advantage in this respect. However, the "Bonn Agreement," which emerged from the most recent round of negotiations of the Kyoto Protocol, now permits industrial nations to gain a limited number of carbon offsets by sponsoring reforestation and afforestation projects in developing countries. A recent study estimated that theoretically feasible reforestation of about 682,000 hectares per year in Africa could absorb about 41.7 metric tons of carbon over the next 10 years (representing 13 percent of the worldwide potential). At a realistic estimate of $10 per metric ton of carbon, this could generate $288.3 million over that period. The Kyoto Protocol does not yet allow offsets based on preventing deforestation of existing forests, or through changing agricultural practices to sequester more carbon in the soil, but this may become a reality in the future. If so, the same study estimates that halting ongoing deforestation of about

312,000 hectares per year in Africa could result in preventing the release of about 167.8 metric tons of carbon between 2003 and 2012 (representing about 11 percent of the total potential for Asia, Africa, and Latin America) and generate $1.28 billion, while improving agricultural practices in about 16 million hectares per year in Africa could sequester an additional 69.7 million metric tons of carbon (18 percent of the total potential) and generate $482 million (Niles forthcoming).

Development Trends and Challenges

Sub-Saharan Africa is a region of diversity and contrasts. Although 65 percent of the continent is arid or semi-arid, it also contains the world's second largest continuous rain forest. Some countries have long stretches of coast, whereas others are land-locked. There are areas of high agricultural potential, such as the eastern African highlands; areas of great mineral wealth, such as the Zambian copper belt and the "diamond coast" of southern Africa; rich marine and freshwater fisheries; and the greatest wildlife tourism attractions in the world. Across the region the population is 70 percent rural, yet the urbanization rate is the highest in the world. This physical, ecological, and social heterogeneity presents challenges and opportunities for achieving sustainable economic development through improved environmental and natural resource management. At the same time, Africa is a region in transition. There are important trends toward decentralization and democratization, as well as a growing demand for transparency and accountability in the management of public assets. The roles of the public sector, the private sector, and civil society at all levels are being redefined; an emphasis on increasing private sector investment and a trend toward subregional integration have the potential for positive impacts on both the people and their environment.

Despite the diversity, a number of common key development trends present challenges and opportunities for environmental management across the region. Depending on how they are managed, these development trends could prove good or bad for Africa's future.

Rapid and Unplanned Urbanization

Urbanization has dramatically transformed Sub-Saharan Africa in recent decades. This demographic shift is already having a major impact on the nature of environmental management challenges in the region, and this impact will grow over the next few decades. While the region's total population has multiplied by 2.5 over the past 30 years, the urban population has increased by a factor of five. Since 1980, it has nearly doubled, from

90 million to 150 million people, with the largest concentrations in South Africa, Nigeria, and the Democratic Republic of Congo. In West Africa, more than 40 percent of the population is now urban. In 1970 only one African city had a population over 1 million; by 1990 there were 18. The majority of the urban population lives in certain coastal areas, which are already densely populated and are continuing to grow rapidly (World Bank 2000b, p. 1). Examples in Africa include the "megalopolis" of more than 50 million people living along 500 kilometers of coastline from Accra to the Niger Delta, sites in South Africa and Mozambique, and port cities of the Horn of Africa. The strain that these megacities will place on existing infrastructure and coastal and marine ecosystems could have serious impacts on local and national economies in terms of lost opportunities, the poor health and productivity of urban populations, and increased vulnerability to natural disasters.

Rapid, uncontrolled urbanization in coastal areas also threatens the tourism industry in many countries, as much of the present and prospective tourism development is in coastal areas. In some areas such as Mombasa, tourism development itself is causing environmental degradation because of inadequate planning and regulation of aspects such as waste disposal and water consumption.

Urbanization can be a positive force for the environment when it reduces pressure on overcrowded or ecologically fragile rural areas or frees up arable land by concentrating dwellings in smaller areas. In many parts of Africa, individual land holdings are already too small to be subdivided further for inheritance, leaving a growing problem of rural landless poor. Urbanization can also reduce demands on local natural resources if the urban settlements import products from a wide area or adopt less resource-demanding technologies, such as cooking with hydropower-generated electricity instead of woodfuels.

However, this does not apply to many African towns and cities, which have been likened to "overgrown villages." A large proportion of urban residents in the most crowded African cities lack the services usually associated with urban centers, such as piped water supply, sanitation, and electricity (see table 2.4). These urban dwellers also remain directly and heavily dependent upon the natural resources of surrounding rural areas, including coastal and near-shore fisheries, forests for woodfuel and building materials, river beds (for building sand), domestic livestock and bushmeat, and so forth. These dense concentrations of consumers can place an enormous strain on the resources of these nearby rural areas, many of which are increasingly unable to support sustainable livelihoods of even the local rural populations.

The "sink" capacity of the environment for wastes is also usually overwhelmed, with few cities having effective sanitation systems. Untreated

Table 2.4. Urban Environment and Services in Selected Cities

City	Urban population (millions) 1995	Urban population (millions) 2015	Average annual growth rate, 1990–95	Urban residential density (persons/hectare), 1993	Poor households (percent)	Urban households connected to water (percent)	Per capita water use (liters/day)	Households connected to sewerage (percent)	Households connected to electricity (percent)	Households with garbage collection (percent)
Ouagadougou	824	2,546	6.5	71	11	32	26	0	35	40
Abidjan	2,793	5,259	4.9	424	37	62	111	45	64	70
Accra	1,673	3,469	3.5	65	25	46	4	23	17	60
Nairobi	1,810	4,228	5.1	93	27	78	116	35	40	47
Antananarivo	876	2,218	4.9	—	32	31	40	17	60	—
Lagos	10,287	24,640	5.7	194	66	65	70	2	100	8
Dakar	1,708	3,489	4.0	—	13	41	69	25	64	75
Addis	2,431	6,578	4.8	314	—	58	27	0	96	2
Kampala	954	2,548	4.7	—	77	30	25	9	42	20
Maputo	2,212	5,306	7.6	191	—	28	80	23	46	37

— Not available.

Note: Cities were selected on the basis of most rapid urbanization rates; data exclude the Republic of South Africa.

Source: World Resources Institute (1998–99).

sewage is returned to water bodies that serve as a source of drinking water and as habitat for vital fish resources. Solid waste accumulates around dwellings, leading to disease and high vermin populations. Drainage systems are also often inadequate or poorly maintained, creating ideal conditions for water-related diseases such as malaria and cholera. Inadequate sanitation is a major cause of the degradation of the quality of the groundwater and surface water. Economic growth leads to larger discharges of wastewater and solid waste per capita. Inadequate investments in waste collection and disposal mean that large quantities of waste enter the groundwater and surface water. Groundwater contamination is less visible but often more serious both because it can take decades for polluted aquifers to cleanse themselves and because large numbers of people drink untreated groundwater.

Outdoor air pollution is a limited and highly localized problem in Africa, compared with other regions. However, the issue is significant in some of the large urban centers with high densities of vehicles (mostly still using diesel and leaded fuel) and low-income settlements located in and around industrial areas.

The interdependence of rural and urban economies is particularly evident in Africa, where town and village households maintain multiple ties through seasonal migration and remittances, creating an informal safety net. Poorly managed urbanization often leads to increased poverty and inequality, which belies the promise of urban development. According to the *Cities in Transition* report (World Bank 2000b), urban poverty is growing in scale and extent in both urban and peri-urban areas. In reality, urban poverty is much broader than economic deprivation; it includes squalid living conditions, risks to life and health from poor sanitation, air pollution, crime and violence, traffic accidents and natural disasters, powerlessness, and the breakdown of traditional family and community safety nets. The poor, and especially poor children, are particularly hurt by a deteriorating urban environment. The urban transition offers significant opportunities for countries to improve the quality of life for all their citizens, and for the Bank to realize its core mission of reducing poverty. But whether this potential is realized depends on the quality of urban management and on the national and local policies affecting it.

Growing Role of the Private Sector

After a long period of mainly state ownership and control of productive enterprises and very poor business environments, most African countries have begun to seek and encourage private sector investment. This can have positive impacts on poverty through economic growth and employment generation. It can also have negative implications, particularly if business enterprises develop by capturing (or degrading) public natural resources for private gain, or if traditionally public services are privatized and move beyond the reach of the poor.

In some cases governments have sought to attract investors by reducing perceived "disincentives," such as environmental or occupational health regulations or standards. This led to serious problems in Mauritius, for example, where inappropriate disposal of dye wastes from the vibrant textile industry threatened coastal waters and, with them, a very lucrative tourism industry.[6] In the current international marketplace, however, there is a growing concern about public image, particularly in relation to environmental and health issues. Serious international investors are increasingly seeking not a fully permissive regulatory environment but a predictable and rational one, in which following good business practices does not put a company at a great disadvantage relative to its less conscientious competitors. The impact of this trend in Africa is less than in some other regions because of the limited amount of international investment overall. However, in some major sectors, such as petroleum and tourism, it does have an impact. Many African countries are also in the process of divesting their publicly owned mines, industrial plants, and the like, on a large scale. The private sector is understandably reluctant to assume the responsibility for potentially large environmental liabilities, for example, from mine-tailings, toxic waste disposal, equipment and processes that do not meet current health and environmental standards, and so forth (see box 2.3). Therefore, the value of maintaining good environmental practice from the beginning is becoming increasingly clear.

Private sector investment in agricultural technology raises issues of particular significance to Africa. Probably the most familiar is the spread of "improved" hybrid crop and livestock varieties. These varieties offer advantages such as higher yields and resistance to certain pests and diseases, but they may not adapt well to the harsh or uncertain climatic conditions and low-input environments that characterize much of smallholder African agriculture. As such, they may prove a risky investment and can reduce livelihood security by displacing better-adapted local varieties. When planted in monoculture over large areas, they are vulnerable to disease epidemics. Commercial crops are usually associated with the heavy use of pesticides, often with negative health and environmental impacts. Recently there has been vigorous debate over genetic engineering of crops, including the introduction of patents for engineered strains and of "terminator genes." Both of these innovations prevent farmers from saving seeds for planting, thus making them entirely dependent on the seed suppliers. Another highly controversial facet of genetic engineering is the incorporation of herbicide resistance or

---

Box 2.3. Addressing Environmental Liabilities in Privatizing State-Owned Entities: Who Picks Up the Tab?

The Ghana Mining Sector Rehabilitation Project supported the rehabilitation and eventual privatization of three state-owned gold mines at Prestea, Dunkwa, and Tarkwa, in the western region of Ghana. Most of the funds were used for operational and safety aspects at the mines, as well as in supporting the enabling policy and institutional framework to assist the government in undertaking the privatization activities. The negotiation process, however, was prolonged, and the prospective joint venture partners were almost losing faith in the divestiture process. One of the issues about which they confronted the government was the environmental liabilities at all three mines. They contended that the government was solely liable for addressing these issues resulting from past mining activities. The International Development Association (IDA) stepped in to facilitate the process and funded environmental audits at all three mines. The audits identified the range of environmental problems at the mines, including the need for tailings dams, reclamation and rehabilitation of mined-out areas, and the provision of water to affected communities.

IDA assisted the government and joint venture partners in negotiating a settlement where the government would use funds from IDA to address the most serious environmental problems. The agreement was that the government had the sole responsibility for environmental issues directly resulting from past mining activities. However, where (a) the private sector partner would benefit from specific improvements and (b) such improvements would add value to the operation of the mine, the private partner should provide matching funding. IDA provided US$1 million for environmental remediation at each of the mines. This funding provided a catalyst for finalizing the agreements for divestiture and eventual privatization. All the privatized mines are operational, and at Tarkwa the private sector has been able to expand the mine's operation. At Prestea, environmental remediation continues with funding from the Nordic Development Fund (NDF), which is a cofinancier with IDA, supporting the follow-on project: the Ghana Mining Sector Development and Environment Project.

---

insecticidal proteins into the genomes of crop plants. Many critics have challenged these technologies as environmentally too risky. At the same time, genetic engineering achievements such as the creation of vitamin-rich "golden rice" have the potential to greatly improve the quality of life of the poor.

Regardless of the sector or type of technology, the challenge is to make the private sector a positive force for the environment. This requires a combination of positive and negative incentives, as well as technical assistance to help businesses respond to these incentives. African countries need support for developing and implementing policies to establish an appropriate business environment, which provides predictable and effective regulation (for example, environmental standards), as well as positive incentives for sound environmental practices such as clean technologies and pollution control measures. They need to build capacity in both the private and public sectors for environmental assessment and audits, and for implementation and monitoring of environmental mitigation plans. This is a particular challenge in Africa because a large proportion of the manufacturing sector is typically composed of small-scale or "informal" enterprises. They have little technical or financial capacity, and perhaps little incentive, to "green" their production systems. Although individually small scale, they can have a large cumulative impact. One important trend is the emergence of "green" investment funds (or "green" windows in broader investment funds) aimed at promoting environmentally related investment in areas such as tourism, recycling-based industries, and alternative energy.

Subregional Integration

One of Sub-Saharan Africa's greatest development challenges is its high degree of political fragmentation. The region is made up of a large number of countries, many of them small and with a limited human, natural, and financial resource base. Some have no direct access to the sea, which is a major constraint given the poorly developed inland transportation infrastructure. Many critical resources span national borders, including rivers and lakes and their watersheds, aquifers, forests, fish stocks and wildlife populations, transport corridors, and coastal currents. Political unrest, natural disasters, and uneven distribution of economic opportunities are not only national but subregional issues, as large numbers of people become transnational migrants or refugees, increasing the pressure on fragile ecosystems and on limited natural and financial resources.

For environmental management, the subregional, rather than the regional, level is the most significant because many ecosystems and natural resources extend over adjacent countries. Many African governments are recognizing the need for cooperation in managing cross-border natural resources, particularly in the wake of recent droughts and floods such as those that afflicted Mozambique, South Africa, and Zimbabwe in 2000. The greatest attention has focused on efforts to coordinate the management and use of shared river basins. Existing initiatives in the region include the Niger Basin Authority, the Lake Chad Basin Commission, and the Nile Basin Initiative. Promotion of regional and subregional cooperation is also one of the 12 focal program areas of the African Ministerial Conference on Environment (AMCEN).

African governments and investors are also interested in economic integration that can help their countries to become more competitive in the world marketplace by harmonizing policies and standards, facilitating free movement of goods, achieving economies of scale in production and marketing, developing diversified tourism products and routes, and the like. While the purpose of subregional organizations such as the Southern Africa Development Community (SADC), the East African Cooperation Community (EACC), and the Economic Community of West African States (ECOWAS) is economic integration and cooperation, this inevitably includes addressing environmental issues. For example, cooperation in water resource management is a particular concern in southern Africa, as 70 percent of the subregion's surface water is shared by two or more member states. Furthermore, serious water shortages are predicted for several of the countries within the next few decades if adequate management measures are not taken. In 1995, the SADC member states signed a Protocol on Shared Watercourse Systems, aimed at equitable sharing of water and ensuring the efficient conservation of the scarce water resource.

Decentralization and Democratization

The political landscape within Africa has been changing rapidly in recent years. Authoritarian regimes of the 1970s and 1980s have been yielding to popular demand for multiparty elections and accountability in public resource management. By 1999 nearly all countries had held multiparty elections with varying degrees of credibility, although the development of accountable, credible, and durable democratic institutions is a longer process. Along with democratization there has been a trend toward decentralization of power and responsibility in a number of areas, including natural resource management. In many countries colonial-era policies and laws, which vested control and management of forests, wildlife, and other resources entirely in the state, are being revised to encompass varying degrees of community ownership or participation ("comanagement"). Sometimes this extends only as far as increasing the role of provincial or district governments (which may just represent extensions of the central government), but in other cases it involves actual devolution to communities or to representative, largely elected bodies. These trends, while internally driven to a large extent, have been bolstered by international aid policies that also emphasize Community-Driven Development and government accountability to domestic stakeholders.

Ideally, democratization improves the allocation and use of natural resources by making the public sector more accountable to civil society. While this may increase the likelihood that resources are used to serve public rather than private interests, it does not necessarily translate to sustainable management or environmental protection. In some countries, such as Malawi, sudden democratization has triggered a widespread public perception that there are no more rules—people are free to grab whatever they can and had better do so before someone else does. Similarly, decentralization is regarded as beneficial because government officials at the local level are closer to the people and therefore should more easily be held accountable by the people for their actions. This is not necessarily true, however, particularly if the officials are appointed rather than elected, or if their constituents are poorly informed. It is also not uncommon for elected officials to encourage their constituents to invade protected areas, violate hunting and fishing laws, and so on, as a means of winning popular support and re-election. To be positive forces for environmental management, democratization and decentralization must be accompanied by education and by appropriate regulatory frameworks.

Community-based natural resource management and environmental management go beyond decentralization to actual devolution of control, and possibly ownership, of resources to the community level. In principle, this puts the power to manage in the hands of those who are most affected when the resources are degraded. It can provide the incentive for sustainable management if the communities can have exclusive access to the resources, including the authority and means to exclude others, and if they have the luxury to make some investments in the future rather than struggling just to meet their immediate needs. In practice, common constraints include internal conflicts (communities generally being composed of different interest groups) and a lack of institutional capacity for cooperative consensus-building, planning, and implementation. This is particularly true where migrations and internal population shifts have brought together people from different ethnic or social backgrounds who have no tradition of working together. It is also difficult to coordinate land or resource use over large areas (for ecosystem management) when the authority is fragmented across many different small communities.

Globalization

Globalization, particularly its impact on the poor in developing countries and on the environment, is one of the most controversial topics in international economics and development today. As with the other major trends, globalization has the potential for both negative and positive consequences at the poverty-environment interface.

One major element of the globalization debate is the increasing domination and control of international and local markets by large, mostly Western-based corporations. This has many economic, social, and environmental implications for developing countries. As discussed above, seeds have become an important focus of the debate that potentially positive impacts of higher yields and improved nutrition are offset by negative impacts such as a narrowing genetic base for major crops, increased dependence on fertilizers and pesticides, and the need for farmers to purchase seeds each year.

Developing countries are pressing for greater access to markets in industrial countries. While this has obvious economic benefits, more accessible global markets for Africa's biological resources present a grave threat of overexploitation. However, this situation is by no means new: tropical timber, commercial fish species, elephant ivory, and other high-value products have always faced this pressure. Similarly, international companies have long been active in Africa, selling products that present environmental and health hazards (highly toxic pesticides, low-quality motor vehicles, hybrid seed varieties that displace local landraces, and the like).

The newer developments of "globalization" include the entry of international interests as investors rather than only as buyers and sellers, and the freer flow of commodities and manufactured products into Africa, where they compete with and can stifle local enterprises. Large, transnational investors can be a positive force, as they are often more concerned about reputational risks than are local companies, and therefore are more likely to heed growing international pressure for good labor practices, reducing environmental impacts, and so forth. The recently approved Chad-Cameroon pipeline is an example. In addition to the need to adhere to the World Bank's Safeguard Policies, the extensive attention paid to environmental and social issues during project preparation reflected the interests of the transnational investors (led by Exxon Mobil) to improve their public image. Key elements of the program include an independent International Advisory Group to monitor compliance with social and environmental safeguards during project implementation; mechanisms to target revenue flows in Chad to key sectors in the country's poverty alleviation strategy; burial of the pipeline and its rerouting to mainly follow existing infrastructure; the creation of two new national parks in Cameroon as "offsets" for the destruction of a small area of tropical forest; and two parallel Bank-financed projects to strengthen Chad's and Cameroon's capacities for environmental management and monitoring of the petroleum sectors.

Transnationals are also more likely to have the resources to respond when a problem arises (for example, cleaning up oil spills or repackaging and destroying or removing stockpiles of obsolete pesticides). Given the interest of most African governments in attracting foreign investment, it is not unusual for transnational companies' internal standards for environmental protection and labor practices to be more exigent than governmental regulations. This is certainly not always the case, however; some transnationals not only take advantage of lax government regulations but also use their economic power to loosen them even further. Nevertheless, international consumer and political pressure is proving increasingly influential, with consumer boycotts, "green certification" schemes, voluntary codes of conduct, and similar instruments. For example, the Global Compact is a United Nations–led initiative to encourage businesses to work with governments and civil society and incorporate into their policies and practices nine principles derived from the Universal Declaration of Human Rights, the Fundamental Principles and Rights at Work of the International Labor Organization, and the Earth Summit-Agenda 21 principles on the environment.[7]

Technology transfer can be a positive outgrowth of globalization, as transnational companies can introduce more energy-efficient and environmentally friendly technologies to replace antiquated production systems often found in African countries. While dedicated technology transfer programs are important, the mere presence of alternatives can be influential: new technologies historically have spread mainly by example and observation (Diamond 1997). There are also risks of introducing potentially harmful technologies, as the ongoing vigorous international debate over genetically modified organisms illustrates.

Another aspect of globalization with potentially positive or negative impacts is the tourism and travel industry, now one of the fastest-growing economic sectors in the world. Tourism is the only export-oriented commercial sector in which Africa's market share is growing. Africa also has a clear comparative advantage in nature-based tourism and "adventure" tourism (perhaps the fastest-growing subsector), where the natural environment is the main attraction (beaches and coral reefs, game-filled savannas, tropical forests, mountains). Environmental management is clearly essential for maintaining this advantage, and the potential for tourism income can provide an important economic rationale for maintaining natural environments. Tourism also generates high levels of employment. However, tourism development itself can also be environmentally and socially destructive, creating pollution, altering natural ecosystems, and undermining traditional livelihoods (for example, large-scale beach tourism development often pollutes coastal waters and displaces fishing villages).

Institutional and Human Resource Capacity Constraints

Institutional and human resource capacities are key to determining how all these development trends will affect environment and poverty. On the whole, Africa's institutions are currently poorly equipped to deal with them because of such factors as inexperience, lack of technical capacity, and lack of transparency and accountability. Institutional and human resource capacity building must target these gaps if the positive potentials of these trends are to be captured and the negative impacts avoided. For example, rapidly growing private sector investment must be managed and steered onto sustainable paths through effective planning, monitoring, regulatory, and incentive structures. In most African countries today the public sector is very weak in these areas. Furthermore, ongoing decentralization of many aspects of financial and natural resource management calls for planning and management capacity at district and local levels, where the "skills gap" is even greater. A history of centralized economies that limited private sector activity, and of inadequate investment in human resource development, has resulted in governments and citizens with a limited capacity to participate in and benefit from private investment opportunities. Strategies for building institutional capacity must also be grounded in other practical realities, such as constrained economies and underpaid civil servants; vested interests with strong political influence; limited human and absorptive capacity, particularly at community and local levels; and a weak or newly emerging private sector.

3

Lessons from World Bank Experience

The Bank's environmental program over the past few decades has included direct investment in environmental improvements and indirect interventions aimed at creating capacity and an enabling environment for better environmental management. Direct investments have included environmental components within sectoral lending operations (for example, urban development, rural development, forestry, agriculture) as well as free-standing environmental projects. In recent years the Bank's main vehicles for "mainstreaming" environment in development programs and building in-country capacity have been National Environmental Action Plans (NEAPs), together with follow-up Environmental Support Programs (ESPs), financed by the Bank and other donors, to support implementation of the actions identified in the NEAPs. Several environmentally related professional and information networks have also grown out of the NEAP process with varying degrees of success. At the community level, mainstreaming of environment has mainly been through community-based natural resource management (CBNRM) programs, which typically include awareness-raising and capacity-building elements as well as modest levels of direct investment in the form of "micro-projects."

The experience gained from these efforts has been mixed, with some promising models and pilot initiatives and important lessons for a forward-looking strategy. Although a detailed discussion is beyond the scope of this paper, the strategy also draws upon the experience of the broader development community in areas such as CBNRM, institutional capacity building, and environmental information.

The main instruments the Bank has used to bring environmental issues into its development support are (a) Environmental Assessment, (b) the Global Environment Facility (GEF), (c) NEAPs, (d) ESPs, (e) regional environmental networks, (f) CBNRM, and (g) Country Assistance Strategies (CASs). Discussions of each instrument follow.

Environmental Assessment

The EA process, now mandated by most donors and governments, has become a powerful tool for ensuring that development actions take into account issues of environmental sustainability and social equity. It also provides an important entry point for incorporating environment into development activities on the ground. Many Bank-financed environmental operations and components originate as elements of Environmental Management Plans (EMPs) developed under the EA process. There have been numerous assessments of the implementation and impact of EA in Africa (see box 3.1). Overall the conclusions from the African experience are very similar to those in other regions, that is, EA is an important but limited tool that (a) can prevent or reduce specific types of environmental damage, but is generally too narrow in scope to deal effectively with secondary, indirect, cumulative, or long impacts; (b) is usually undertaken too late in the project cycle to influence design except at the margins; and (c) rarely includes adequate follow-up to ensure implementation and to evaluate the success of proposed mitigation measures called for in the EMPs.

One recent development with major operational implications was the introduction of the independent "Inspection Panel," which enables organizations and private citizens to challenge how the Bank applies its Safeguard Policies in specific cases. While a grievance mechanism is important for transparency and can result in improvements in performance and sustainability of investments, it also absorbs a great deal of staff time that could otherwise be devoted to improving the overall EA process. It can also lead to risk-averse behavior such as avoiding Bank involvement in projects that are regarded as likely to trigger an appeal to the Inspection Panel or the ill-advised reorientation of project designs in an effort to make them "Inspection Panel–proof."

Observations such as those from the 1995 review have led to a greater focus on the EMP, which outlines the mitigating and monitoring activities to be undertaken and by whom, as well as measures to enhance the implementers' capacity for environmental review and monitoring. Making the EMP an integral part of project design and implementation, including referencing it in project legal agreements, provides greater assurance that the mitigation measures will be carried out. To address the capacity issue, Bank projects have helped strengthen the authorities responsible for implementing EA legislation in many countries. The Bank is also supporting a regional initiative, the Capacity Development and Linkages for Environmental Impact Assessment in Africa, which aims to help every African country have a functional system in place, adapted to

Box 3.1. The World Bank and Environmental Assessment

A 1995 review of EA in the Africa Region since 1989 reached the following conclusions:

- Progress in EA in Africa has been significant during this 15-year period, with EA legislation now existing in more than half of the countries, although human and technical resources for implementation are often inadequate. For example, insufficient resources are being mobilized for the field supervision of Bank-financed projects. Coordination among donors is also still far from satisfactory, and there is limited experience in monitoring environmental impacts in the field.
- The EA process is hampered by a lack of financial support and insufficient dialogue among assessors, governments, and other stakeholders. The general weaknesses of national institutions and the scarcity of trained African EA specialists have added to the difficulties.
- EA preparation has not included enough decisionmaking tools like Geographic Information Systems (GIS) and environmental economics.
- The Environmental Review process is fully effective at present on only a limited part of the Bank's portfolio. In particular, there has been insufficient integration into structural adjustment instruments as well as strategic documents such as Country Assistance Strategies.
- EAs have contributed to improved project design through increased capacity building and monitoring, and have, for example, improved management of involuntary resettlement in many cases.

The assessment recommended increased assistance for capacity and institution building, development and dissemination of improved tools and methods, improved communication and awareness building, and promotion of "win-win" solutions such as the use of clean technologies and renewable energy.

Source: Mercier (1995).

the local needs and capacity, by 2010. Similarly, country-specific projects and regional technical networks have been put in place to help improve the availability and use of tools such as Environmental Information Systems and environmental economics.

Whereas some progress has been made on the first three issues identified in the 1995 review, there has been relatively little progress on the fourth. To capture its full potential, EA must evolve from a reactive mechanism for avoiding negative impacts to a positive, proactive planning tool. This is particularly important as the Bank continues to increase its use of non-project-lending instruments such as sectoral investment programs, budget support (including Structural Adjustment Loans [SALs], Poverty Reduction Strategy Credit [PRSC], and Public Expenditure Review Credit [PERC]), and Community-Driven Development initiatives. The project-specific EA model is a poor fit with these types of operations. Environmental practitioners are therefore promoting the use of Strategic Environmental Assessments (SEAs), which go beyond the project-by-project approach. The Bank is committed to moving in this direction (as outlined in the WBES), but so far there are few accepted procedures or experiences to draw upon. However, some SEAs have been undertaken, including a few in Africa (such as an SEA for the water sector in Zambia), and efforts are being made to integrate EA into structural adjustment lending, PRSCs, and Community Action Programs (see box 3.2). Another issue the Bank is tackling is how to apply EA to projects in which funds are used to capitalize financial intermediaries, rather than being disbursed directly by the Bank for pre-identified activities.

Aside from these technical issues, one of the main dilemmas of EA is that clients still often regard it (along with many of the Bank's other Safeguard Policies) as an externally imposed "conditionality" and obstacle, rather than as a means to improve the quality and impact of projects. This in part accounts for the typically poor execution of EMPs and the lack of impact monitoring during implementation.

All of this highlights the need to emphasize building of constituency, commitment, and capacity in-country, rather than simply ensuring compliance with the Bank's Safeguard Policies in Bank-financed operations. Bank-financed projects and policy dialogue have encouraged and helped many African governments to enact EA laws and regulations. This is a positive development, but some problems still often arise (for example, overly bureaucratic and cumbersome procedures that can lead developers to circumvent the process whenever possible, inadequate financial and human resources to prepare and review EAs, and a lack of resources or even procedures or legal mandates to enforce implementation of mitigation measures or monitor impacts). In keeping with its policy and strategy of facilitating private sector–led growth, the Bank is trying to expand the scope of awareness raising and capacity building for EA to a wider range of stakeholders and actors.

The Global Environment Facility

Many bilateral donors are willing to provide grant funding to African countries for environmental initiatives. However, having a source of dedicated grant funds administered by the Bank itself has been very useful for introducing environmental elements into Bank-financed programs

---

Box 3.2. Integrating Safeguard Policies into Community Action Programs

A pilot study (for Bank-wide application) is being conducted in the Africa Region to ensure smooth and cost-effective integration of the 10 Safeguard Policies into the new Community Action Programs (CAPs, also known as Community-Driven Development [CDD]). Contrary to common belief, community-based projects can present a significant risk of environmental harm if they are not planned and managed properly. Water, agriculture, forestry, and infrastructure projects in particular require attention. Broad-scale programs implemented through numerous small community projects can have cumulative impacts (for example, communities may deplete forests for firewood to bake bricks for building schools), and even single micro-subprojects can have harmful local effects (for example, latrine effluent seeping into a source of drinking water).

CDD/CAPs will be treated as the EA-category Financial Intermediaries —a category introduced by the Operational Policy/Bank Procedures/Good Practice 4.01 in February 1999—implying that the Safeguard Policies should be integrated in the same way as projects implemented through Financial Intermediaries. Thus, the capacity of communities and local governments in environmental assessment and management needs to be gradually strengthened. Two pilot case studies are being started: one on an ongoing urban project (Senegal) and one on a rural project (Chad) still in preparation.

The final report of this study includes recommendations on standard terms of reference for EAs of CAPs, as well as the design and comparisons of various models of capacity and institution building and of monitoring systems for putting in place and maintaining the mechanisms needed to screen the subprojects generated by the CAPs and submit them to Environmental and Social Assessments.[8]

---

and operations that might not otherwise include them. A substantial proportion of Bank-financed natural resource management operations in Africa now include GEF-financed components. There have been difficulties, such as a lack of understanding of GEF objectives and processes and a lack of client and stakeholder (and Bank) support and ownership for what are sometimes regarded as low-priority projects that do not address poverty or contribute to economic development. In response, the Bank's (and more broadly GEF's) strategy has been to seek "win-win" opportunities for interventions that address both global and local objectives, and to reduce the number of free-standing GEF projects. The most common are community-based land and natural resource management projects that also aim to promote biodiversity conservation and/or carbon storage. Blended GEF/World Bank projects are appealing from the perspective of ownership and leverage, but they can run into processing problems, such as diverging time frames, as the GEF component requires additional steps in processing and approval. Some Task Teams are reluctant to integrate GEF components too fully into Bank-financed operations because of the risk that approval of the GEF element may be delayed or even denied, leaving a hole in the project concept. Another approach to increasing client ownership of GEF projects has been supporting the preparation of National Biodiversity Conservation Strategies and Plans (NBCSPs), with the aim of ensuring that projects proposed for GEF support reflect identified national priorities. While this has sometimes been useful, many African countries have not completed NBCSPs, and those that have been completed do not always give clear guidance with respect to national priorities or commitment.

National Environmental Action Plans

NEAPs have been prepared by almost all African countries over the past 10 to 15 years (along with all other IDA countries, in response to a requirement set out for IDA 10 financing). A recent World Bank Operations Evaluation Department (OED) evaluation (Shilling 2001) concluded that the process of preparing NEAPs helped build within countries awareness of and consensus on the importance of environmental issues, but their impact to date in terms of improving environmental management capacity and performance has been fairly limited. Another review[9] examined the process and impacts of NEAPs and follow-up Environmental Support Programs, combining a general overview with case studies on three countries (Benin, The Gambia, and Uganda) that had completed NEAPs and are now implementing them through ESPs financed at least in part by the World Bank. The latter study echoed the positive conclusions regarding the role of NEAPs with respect to in-country building awareness (putting environment on the national agenda, at least briefly), and stimulating participatory processes and dialogue between the public sector and other stakeholders. However, it also noted that in many countries in which NEAPs were regarded as externally driven and undertaken only to meet an IDA requirement, governments displayed little real ownership and commitment to the NEAPs. As a result, these countries have done little follow-up after the document was completed and approved by the Bank.

Overall, NEAPs have enhanced the visibility of environment, strengthened environmental institutions, and supported some positive

investment, but they have generally not succeeded in making environmental sustainability a core objective in countries' development agendas.
In fact, it may be argued that by establishing a distinct NEAP process separate from overall development planning, and by supporting dedicated
environmental projects implemented mainly by environmental agencies,
NEAPs and ESPs have contributed to isolating the environmental agenda
from the mainstream of development (World Bank 2000c).

Environmental Support Programs

About one-third of the countries that prepared NEAPs in African countries have implemented ESPs based on them (six of them financed at least
in part by the Bank). The ESPs have mostly focused on putting in place
the policy, legal, and institutional reforms recommended under the
NEAPs. They also aim to adjust or supplement ongoing sectoral programs and projects to help make them consistent with the policies and
strategies articulated in the NEAP. In general, donor support provided
through the ESPs targets the following:

• Institutional development and capacity building
• Development of policy, legal, and regulatory frameworks
• Generation and management of environmental information
• Biodiversity conservation and protected areas management
• Community-based and decentralized environmental management ini-
  tiatives
• Environmental education, public awareness and communication, and
  research programs.

The ESPs provide limited lessons because most are relatively new and
the institutional development and other impacts they seek take time to
come to fruition. In all three case studies covered by the recent
NEAP/ESP review, however, the review concluded that there has been
success in developing a "functional institutional, policy and regulatory
framework" built mainly upon a central environmental agency and EA
legislation and regulations. It also pointed to success in improving information systems and datasets and gave examples of how they have influenced policy and development decisions.

The review also notes that the rate of implementation of ESPs is generally quite slow because of the limited technical, administrative, and
managerial capacity in the countries in both the public and private sectors. Skills had to be developed in EA, pollution control, information
systems, and the like, before other aspects of the projects could really be
implemented. The responsibility for administering and coordinating

multisectoral ESPs has in some cases overwhelmed environmental agencies, preventing them from carrying out other important functions such as continuing policy and strategy development. Capacity building within most ESPs has emphasized the public sector, neglecting the equally important need to build capacity in the private sector and civil society (for example, NGOs). In addition, while most of the NEAPs and ESPs stress the objective of decentralizing environmental and natural resource management to district, local, and community levels, they have not paid enough attention to building the necessary capacity at these levels. The report notes that the overall lack of monitoring and evaluation of the impact of ESPs is due in large part to the difficulty of identifying suitable interim indicators. It also recommends greater use of participatory monitoring and evaluation as one means of increasing the relevance and ownership of ESPs on the part of their wide range of stakeholders.

The review identifies financial sustainability as a major issue, noting that in many cases donors (including the Bank) are providing far greater funding for these environmental agencies than the governments would normally have provided. This often includes generous staff salaries and a substantial investment in equipment, creating a situation that is highly aid-dependent and unsustainable.

The two most important strategic conclusions of reviews of NEAPs and ESPs are the following: (a) the time frame for ESPs (typically five to six years) is too short, given that human resource and institutional capacity must be built up before implementation of other aspects can even begin, and (b) the model of environmental capacity building must evolve in light of important changes occurring in Africa, particularly changes in the role of the state. Institutional and skills development needs to focus on assisting the public sector to act as a facilitator rather than a "doer" and "controller," and on the capacity of all stakeholders to participate in partnerships for environmental management.

Regional Environmental Networks

During the period when many African countries were preparing NEAPs, the Bank facilitated the development of a network for information exchange and mutual support among environmental professionals (mostly government officials) involved in the NEAP process. Over several years this has evolved into the Network for Environment and Sustainable Development in Africa (NESDA), and has also spun off several other professional networks focused on specific elements of NEAP implementation and environment in general (environmental information, environmental economics, and local environmental management, such as the MELISSA [Managing Environment Locally in Sub-Saharan Africa] program and network). A number of other networks also operate in Africa, such as the biodiversity strategies network in southern Africa, the West African Enterprise Network (WAEN), and the Sustainable Use Network of the World Conservation Union. These networks often have high technical quality, but questions have arisen regarding their constituency, ownership, and sustainability once donor funding ends. One approach has been to try to spin off the project management unit into an independent entity, such as an NGO, which can then seek funding from its membership, donors, or contracts. The membership of some networks, including NESDA, is primarily made up of and run by environmental professionals in public service institutions, perhaps in part because they have the greatest access to donor support to meet travel and equipment costs. Building academic or private sector membership is more difficult in Africa than in many other regions because of the financial constraints of academic institutions and the weakness of the private sector, particularly in environmental service fields. Moving to a "user community model" with broader membership may be essential for the effectiveness and sustainability of these networks, but it will be difficult to achieve unless membership confers clear career or commercial benefits, such as access to professional (for example, consulting) opportunities.

Community-Based Natural Resource Management

CBNRM provides a people-centered framework for responding to priority environmental problems. It also helps to mobilize communities and enable them to become more effective players in political and economic decisionmaking processes. It empowers communities not only by improving their access to natural resources but, in many cases, by establishing or strengthening their rights to use and control access to those resources. It also supports other important objectives such as participatory approaches and accountability. This is enhanced even further as CBNRM programs are in some cases evolving into Community-Driven Development (CDD) programs, in which communities have much greater freedom and flexibility to make their own decisions in managing and allocating resources, including money from externally financed "Social Funds."

Lessons can be learned from the problems that have emerged in the implementation of CBNRM approaches. The heart of a CBNRM project is usually some type of Community Action Plan (CAP) in which community members identify priority issues and activities for the project to support. This CAP is often developed through a Participatory Rural

Appraisal (PRA) process, facilitated by the project sponsor. However, the PRA is not necessarily a good instrument for encouraging communities to define a sustainable, self-help-oriented natural resource management agenda. The output of a typical PRA is typically a long "wish list" of investments activities with an emphasis on social infrastructure to meet immediate needs, such as schools, clinics, boreholes, and the like. While some natural resource or environmental management–related activities usually also appear, they tend to be given relatively low priority by the community members but high priority by the sponsor. This can lead to mutual frustration. A PRA also tends to focus attention on proximate and short-term solutions rather than on addressing underlying issues. For example, it may identify fertilizers, a borehole, or an irrigation system as a priority development need while overlooking deeper issues such as land security or depletion of the water table. Community resource mapping exercises tend to produce better results from this standpoint, as they focus attention on identifying natural resource availability and constraints.

The most common shortcomings of CBNRM projects are (a) allowing too little time for truly participatory preparation and to enable underlying and long-term issues to emerge; (b) providing inadequate up-front support for strengthening the capacity of communities to participate effectively in project design and implementation; and (c) building dependency rather than self-sufficiency by trying to solve problems mainly through externally funded "micro-projects" rather than assisting communities to mobilize their own resources. Box 3.3 gives an example of a CBNRM-oriented project, currently in preparation, which incorporates some of these lessons.

Country Assistance Strategies, Poverty Reduction Strategies, and Mainstreaming

In addition to their in-country role, NEAPs were meant to provide the basis for integrating environment into the Bank's Country Assistance Strategies (CASs), which play a central role in shaping the more detailed Bank interventions. Several recent reviews (Ekbom and Bojö 1997; Shilling 2001; Shyamsundar and others 2001) generally concluded that environment has made some inroads into CASs, in stiff competition with other priorities. However, most CASs still treat environment as a sector, with separate funding, objectives, activities, and the like, rather than a cross-cutting theme affecting all sectors. The OED report (Shilling 2001) also notes that overall few specific NEAP findings and recommendations have been integrated into CASs. However, there is considerable variation in the quality of treatment given to environmental matters, and therefore

Box 3.3. Improving Livelihoods through Promoting Sound Management of Microwatersheds in Nigeria

The Nigeria Microwatershed and Environmental Management Project (under development) supports community-managed investments in microwatersheds in six states within three macrowatersheds in Nigeria: the Niger Trough, Upper Benue Trough, and Anambra/Imo Trough. The project supports direct investments at the community level to promote sustainable management of natural resources. The investments may include activities to mitigate gully erosion, reforestation, basic water supply and sanitation, and environmental education. The program aims to decentralize decisionmaking authority for prioritizing activities and also financial resources for implementation to community associations. The project would also provide support to the federal, state, and local levels of government to (a) develop an enabling environment, (b) reduce the potential for conflict among stakeholders, (c) provide the required incentives for long-term investments, and (d) develop capacity at all levels for environmental assessments. The project will also promote partnerships and collaborative arrangements in wildlife and biodiversity management, including incentives for promoting sustainable use of biodiversity. Direct program benefits are expected to include (a) decreased soil erosion (land degradation) on upland areas; (b) reduction in downstream floods; (c) increased production of fodder, woodfuels, and grasses; (d) increased agricultural productivity on arable lands; and (e) improved management and use of biodiversity and natural habitats. The project's special emphasis on women and vulnerable groups within the target watersheds is expected to lead to empowerment of these groups and to improvement of their economic and social conditions.

scope for learning from examples of best practice (see box 3.4). The same can be said of integrating environment into Poverty Reduction Strategies, which are becoming the basis for preparation of CASs in the future (see box 3.5).

Mainstreaming of environment also remains a challenge at the sectoral level. Progress has been made in some key sectors, such as forestry and energy, where mainstreaming has been supported by Bank-wide policies. In others, however, environmental issues continue to be regarded as related primarily to the environmental Safeguard Policies and sometimes treated as burdensome "add-ons." The agricultural and rural development sectors are particularly significant in terms of the impact on environmental management in Africa. Issues such as soil conservation and agroforestry have been significantly internalized within the rural devel-

---

Box 3.4. The 1998 Country Assistance Strategy for Lesotho

The 1998 Lesotho CAS has been cited as an example of good practice in integrating environment into a country assistance strategy. It identifies increased environmental degradation as one of the fundamental constraints to economic growth and discusses the need to manage poverty-related environmental degradation, particularly the loss of soil fertility and productive pasture land and the occurrence of environmental disasters such as droughts and floods.

The section on "Focus of Bank Assistance" states that the Bank will support "a comprehensive approach to the natural resource environment; ensure conservation of natural resources and protection of the environment, especially land degradation, through support for the Government's environmental action plan, agricultural sector development strategy, water management systems, and population planning."

Specific support (complementing support for NEAP implementation being provided by other donors, such as the United Nations Development Programme [UNDP]) includes water supply and sanitation, biodiversity conservation linked with tourism development, and range management and land reform through a Policy Reform and Capacity Building Project for Agriculture.

---

opment agenda, but others, such as integrated pest management and the conservation of genetic diversity of crops, have received less attention. In some cases this may be because these objectives are (wrongly) perceived as going counter to the core objectives of intensifying and modernizing agricultural production. Overall, the management of specific natural resources such as trees, pastures, and water sources has been integrated as a core element in sustainable rural development, but the concept of maintaining a well-functioning agro-ecosystem has not. In all sectors, there are clear opportunities for better mainstreaming of environment (see box 4.1).

Box 3.5. Burkina Faso Poverty Reduction Strategy Paper

The Burkina Faso Poverty Reduction Strategy Paper (PRSP) is based on seven major principles, including sustainable development of natural resources. Key links between poverty and environment are identified, especially land degradation leading to low yields and therefore to poverty. The urban poor cite "climate-related hazards" as a major concern, indicating a high degree of vulnerability to natural forces.

With agriculture identified as the major economic sector, the PRSP notes that short fallow periods, inadequate use of fertilizers, overgrazing, and woodfuel harvesting contribute directly to degradation of the vegetative cover. The country's climatic conditions, land-locked status, and low agricultural productivity, coupled with degradation of soil and water, are seen as the major constraints to economic growth and contribute to massive poverty and food insecurity.

The PRSP states that particular attention must be paid to preventing soil degradation and preserving soil fertility in the context of actions for promoting agricultural growth, and that one of these actions will be rehabilitation of degraded lands. It calls for promotion of soil and water conservation techniques, as currently only 15 percent and 8 percent of farms apply erosion control and agroforestry, respectively. Land ownership is also to be made more secure to encourage better land management. However, the paper does not note that this type of agricultural development can be a double-edged sword from an environmental perspective. Higher profits in agriculture will create incentives and resources for soil and water conservation, but they may also lead to cultivation of fragile lands, salinization of irrigation areas, and increased use of pesticides.

Inadequate water supply and sanitation, links to waterborne diseases, and poor health among the poor are also emphasized. Since 1995 the Ministry of Environment and Water has been responsible for the cross-cutting agenda of enhancing water quality for the poor.

Economic growth is also expected to be fueled by an expansion of mining, industry, and tourism. Making the economy "more attractive for investors" and "simplifying red tape needed to establish an enterprise" are laudable objectives. However, no mention is made of the need for adequate Environmental Assessment as part of this process.

4
Priorities for Action

Thematic Priorities

The World Bank Environment Strategy (WBES) organizes priorities for action within three broad categories: improving (a) the quality of life, (b) the quality of growth, and (c) the quality of the global commons. In Africa these categories tend to blend together, inextricably linked through the common denominator of the region's renewable natural resources. These resources form the basis for both the day-to-day lives of the majority of African people and the region's main prospects for economic growth and development. At the same time, the international community regards Africa's indigenous biological resources and its multinational water bodies as important elements of the "global commons."

Based on the WBES organizing framework, the Africa Region Environment Strategy (ARES) emphasizes the following areas:

a. Quality of life—means enhancing natural resource–based livelihoods through sustainable management of soils, water, and biological resources; protecting peoples' health from environmental burdens including pollution and environmentally related diseases; and reducing peoples' vulnerability to environmental risks and natural disasters.
b. Quality of growth—highlights the need to establish an enabling institutional environment; specifically, this means strengthening the regulatory, incentive, and institutional frameworks needed to promote and support environmentally sustainable, private sector–led economic growth.
c. Quality of the global commons—prioritizes subregional and regional cooperation in management of shared environmental resources; strengthens African countries' capacity to predict and adapt to impacts of climate change; and assists African countries in participating in international efforts to achieve global environmental objectives and to capture a greater share of emerging markets for global environmental services.

Subregional Priorities

Africa is so diverse ecologically and socially that only very general priorities can be defined at a continent-wide level. For more specific analysis, the continent is usually divided into six subregions characterized by similar environmental conditions and socioecological challenges and priorities for environmental action to alleviate poverty. These are the Sudano-Sahelian Belt, humid West Africa, the Congo Basin, East Africa, southern Africa, and the Indian Ocean Islands (World Bank 1996).[10] The following section outlines the highest priorities for environmental management for each subregion, emphasizing issues that affect the livelihoods, health, and security of the poor; opportunities for economic development based on environmental resources; and unique global assets under threat. Some issues, such as land degradation, are equally significant across the continent, whereas others, such as coastal zone management and water scarcity, are more localized.

The most urgent environmental issues and needs identified for each subregion are as follows:

Sudano-Sahelian Belt. Drought preparedness, integrated water resource management, halting or reversal of land degradation (desertification), sustainable woodfuel supply, migratory pest outbreaks

Humid West Africa. Integrated coastal zone management (particularly from Côte d'Ivoire to Nigeria, where one-third of the population lives in coastal areas), including both sustainable management of fisheries resources and urban and industrial environmental waste management and sanitation; land tenure and land management; conservation of the remaining primary rainforest; and protection of the high watersheds of major river systems (particularly in the Central African Republic, Guinea, and Sierra Leone)

Congo Basin. Meeting of peoples' needs and development aspirations while conserving the second largest contiguous primary tropical rainforest in the world, through a combination of core protected areas and improved management of forest production areas; coastal zone management, particularly in areas with intense urban development

East Africa. Reversal of land degradation resulting from inappropriate agricultural practices, particularly in arid/semi-arid areas; integrated water resource management in areas of growing local scarcity; insurance of the sustainability and broadening of the benefits of nature-based tourism, including maintaining critical wildlife habitats and managing human/wildlife conflicts; urban and industrial environmental management in coastal areas

Southern Africa. Water resource conservation and management, drought preparedness and adjustment to climate variability, land tenure, balancing of agricultural development and maintenance of biodiversity resources for tourism development and for global significance, urban environmental management in highly urbanized and rapidly urbanizing areas, meeting of energy requirements

Indian Ocean Islands. Reversal of land degradation; intensification of efforts to protect unique biodiversity, pollution control, and industrial environmental management for public health and for compatibility with tourism; adaptation to climate change.

Even a subregional breakdown is too broad to give a full picture, as particular countries or even areas within countries will have their own urgent priorities that must emerge from country- and location-specific analysis and consultation. For example, environmental and health impacts of wastes and emissions from mining of copper, gold, aluminum, and other minerals may be the most urgent environmental issue in certain parts of some countries.

Sectoral Priorities

While environment is intrinsically cross-sectoral, most governments, donor organizations, and development programs are organized along sectoral lines. Therefore, most direct environmental action will have to be achieved through integrating the environmental agenda into sectoral strategies, policies, and programs: in other words, by ensuring that environmental soundness and sustainability become integral objectives within these sectors and are recognized as important elements of success. This includes finding suitable entry points and synergies with existing sectoral strategies (see box 4.1). Sectors targeted for their strong significance to environmental management include agriculture and rural development, natural resource management (including water, mineral and biological resources), energy, urban development, transport, health, and private sector development (including tourism).

Based on the strategic documents described in box 4.1 and others, table 4.1 proposes the priority environmental issues for key sectors.

Box 4.1. Environmental Entry Points for Some Key Sectoral Strategies

Rural Development. The Bank's Rural Development (RD) Strategy for Africa focuses on increasing rural incomes, aiding service delivery to improve both the quality of life and income generation (for example, inputs, credit, infrastructure), and reducing risk. Agriculture is regarded as the main engine of growth because of the important forward and backward linkages, and certain aspects of environment, such as soil fertility and vegetative cover, are recognized as significant factors in maintaining agricultural productivity. Productivity gains are to be achieved by increasing land and labor productivity—by increasing inputs where land is the main constraint and increasing financial and capital inputs where labor is the constraint. Operationally, there is an ongoing shift from direct investment in assisting growth in agricultural productivity to indirect interventions such as strengthening institutions, improving the efficiency of factor markets (seed supply, land reform), improving access to markets (through information and infrastructure), and reforming agricultural policy. Risk reduction is seen as key because unmanaged risk pushes people back down into poverty. Some major sources of risk for the poor are isolation, environmental degradation, and disease.

Energy. In *Fuel for Thought,* the World Bank (2000d) has articulated a clear strategy around the multifaceted interface between energy and environment. It emphasizes reforming the energy sector, improving supply- and demand-side efficiency through pricing reform and other means, accelerating the substitution of traditional fuels by modern energy, promoting new energy technologies (including renewables) by removing barriers to the development of their markets, and strengthening monitoring and enforcement of mitigation of environmental impacts of energy production and use. In urban and peri-urban areas, Bank support will focus on improving the efficiency of energy utilities and promoting improvements in end-use efficiency. In rural areas, it will focus on developing and mainstreaming new solutions to the challenge of expanding access to modern energy services, including renewables, and on more sustainable management and efficient utilization of traditional fuels. Another important aspect of the strategy is selectivity—supporting investments in the energy sector of countries that have shown a commitment to improving sector efficiency through policy reform and/or sector restructuring, and supporting private sector investment in cases where this can support the momentum toward efficiency gains through further sector reform. In addition to this Bank-wide energy/environment strategy, the Africa Region has developed a Renewable (Nontraditional) Energy Strategy for Africa (RESA). The RESA emphasizes decentralized rural electrification

(DRE), with a large element of renewable energy technologies, such as solar photovoltaic and thermal sources, as these are often the least-cost solution for DRE.

Water Resources. The water resources management strategy is based on the principle that water is a scarce good with dimensions of economic efficiency, social equity, and environmental sustainability (Sharma and others 1996). It recommends an integrated, cross-sectoral, catchment area approach to water resources management in African countries and identifies five priority areas: household water security, catchment area and wetland protection (environmental stewardship, food security, water quality and human health, intranational and international cooperation, and conflict resolution.

Private Sector Development. The Bank's Africa Region strategy identifies four essential dimensions: securing the economic and infrastructural foundations (macroeconomic stability, liberalized markets for trade and investment, alleviation of power, water, telecommunications, and transport constraints that hamper business activity); strengthening the institutional underpinning of markets (refocusing public institutions to become more supportive of private sector development through reducing transaction costs and the risks of doing business); building business capacity, particularly among indigenous small and medium-size enterprises; and developing robust financial systems. It further recommends that in most countries the Bank should focus its efforts on entry points in five key areas: private participation in infrastructure, agribusiness, manufacturing and other urban commercial activity, extractive industries, and tourism. Like the energy strategy, it stresses selectivity, including prioritizing the agenda within countries as well as directing efforts and resources toward those countries that demonstrate a political commitment to helping themselves and instituting necessary economic reforms (World Bank 1994).

Cross-Cutting Priorities

People-Focused Ecosystem Management

The issues and priorities presented above are not new. In fact, most have been the focus of many strategies and programs, but the continued and even accelerating rate of environmental degradation demonstrates that we have not yet succeeded in addressing them. This highlights the need for the Bank and its clients to pursue new approaches and paradigms.

Table 4.1. Priority Sectors and Sectoral Issues

Sector	Priorities for improved environmental management
Macroeconomic policy and planning	Integrating environment into Poverty Reduction Strategies, Country Assistance Strategies, and budget support operations
	Collecting and analyzing country-specific, geo-referenced data to elucidate the linkages between environmental degradation and poverty and to identify and monitor environmental assets that are essential for sustainable development
	Realigning economic policies to remove perverse subsidies and provide incentives for sustainable resource management
	Reorienting development planning to give appropriate consideration to maintaining strategic environmental assets (e.g., important watersheds)
Agriculture	Ensuring environmentally sustainable agricultural intensification (including soil fertility management, integrated pest management, and farming systems; meeting international trade standards)
	Improving land administration and land tenure
	Maintaining crop and livestock genetic diversity and indigenous biodiversity in agricultural systems
	Managing irrigation (including restoration of salinized soils)
	Improving extension and dissemination of environmentally sound methods
	Matching economic development to environmental conditions and sustainable capacity (e.g., removing artificial incentives that encourage agriculture in drought-prone areas)
	Adapting to climate change (including improved medium- and long-term weather predictions)
	Developing policies on the introduction and use of genetically modified organisms

Renewable natural resource management (forests, rangelands, fisheries, wildlife, etc.)	Removing perverse policy incentives (and power structures) that favor nonsustainable exploitation
	Addressing resource tenure issues and community-based natural resource management
	Maintaining biodiversity in utilization areas (e.g., exploited natural forests, plantations, heavily fished waters, areas of livestock and wildlife conflict)
	Shifting economic systems from exploitation of natural biological assets to production (e.g., aquaculture, plantations, and woodlots), without displacing or degrading natural habitats
Nonrenewable natural resource management (mining)	Controlling and containing toxic effluents, emissions, and waste products
	Introducing and disseminating more environmentally friendly mining and refining processes
	Cleaning up severely toxic and highly hazardous mine sites
	Managing environmental liabilities in privatization processes
Urban development, water supply, and sanitation	Improving infrastructure and services in water supply, drainage, waste collection, etc. (with user participation and cost recovery for sustainability)
	Undertaking integrated urban planning, with attention to environmental conditions (e.g., discouraging dense settlements in environmentally fragile or risky areas)
	Setting and enforcing standards
	Providing environmental and hygiene education
	Performing risk assessment and disaster management planning
Health	Providing water and sanitation services and hygiene education

(Table continues on the following page.)

Table 4.1. (continued)

Sector	Priorities for improved environmental management
	Providing environmentally sound vector control
	Improving woodstoves and indoor ventilation
	Managing biohazard waste management
	Ensuring occupational health and safety
	Maintaining biological resources and a knowledge base for traditional medicine
Energy	Providing a sustainable woodfuel supply
	Managing community-based woodlands and woodlots
	Developing alternative domestic energy sources
	Managing watershed and water resources for hydropower
	Reducing biodiversity and socioeconomic impacts of dams
Transport	Reducing primary and secondary environmental impacts of roads
	Improving port management, including reducing chronic and acute oil spillage
	Reducing particulate air pollution and vehicle-based lead burden in major cities[a]
Private sector development	Establishing transparent, equitable, and predictable regulatory regimes with realistic standards reliably enforced
	Building environmental assessment and environmental management capacity (in large, medium, and small enterprises)
	Providing economic incentives and technology transfer for environmentally friendly manufacturing and procurement
	Developing environmentally sound tourism
	Dealing with environmental liabilities in privatization

Containing and ecologically restoring hazardous sites (especially mining sites)

Community-Driven Development	Raising awareness and building capacity for environmental management at the community level
	Subsidizing or otherwise encouraging the use of community funds and resources for environmental management[b] (e.g., reduced matching requirements, earmarked funds)

a. Note, however, that in most cases, leaded fuel is probably not the major source of lead burden affecting African people.
b. This is needed to overcome the natural tendency to "discount" environmental issues as less immediate than other needs.

Perhaps the most significant is the need to move to an ecosystem-based approach to environmental management and development.

An ecosystem is a community of interacting organisms and the physical environment in which they live. In geographic terms, it is an area defined by ecological functions rather than administrative boundaries. Actions affecting any part of an ecosystem affect the whole, and a breakdown of any element can have repercussions for the entire system. The ecosystem is therefore the logical operational unit for environmental management. Beyond this, these ecosystems provide the base for livelihoods and economic development in Africa, and this base is rapidly eroding (see box 4.2). To reverse this catastrophic process, the ecosystem paradigm must be extended beyond environmental management to become the underlying framework for development in the region.

Integrated ecosystem management (IEM) is not just a theoretical construct but is becoming widely accepted and adopted as the keystone of the environmental action agenda. The Global Environment Facility (GEF) has endorsed the IEM approach under its latest Operational Program (Integrated Ecosystems and Natural Resource Management) and now looks for evidence of an IEM approach in virtually all proposals. Major international environmental organizations such as the World Wildlife Fund, the Nature Conservancy, and the African Wildlife Foundation have formally adopted the IEM approach, as has the United States government, among others (Council on Environmental Quality 1993, chapter 6). The African Ministerial Conference on Environment (AMCEN) has also structured its agenda along ecosystem lines (see box 1.1).

Most recently, the report *World Resources 2000–2001: People and Ecosystems, The Fraying Web of Life* (World Resources Institute 2000) highlighted the need to halt the deterioration of the major ecosystems that provide us with food, fiber, energy, and all the essentials of life. In the foreword to this report, the president of the World Bank, the administrator of the United Nations Development Programme, the executive-director of the United Nations Environment Programme, and the president of WRI stated: "If we choose to continue our current patterns of use, we face almost certain declines in the ability of ecosystems to yield their broad spectrum of benefits . . . .The poor, who often depend directly on ecosystems for their livelihoods, suffer most when ecosystems are degraded." In endorsing the report, these heads of agencies "reconfirm their commitment to making the viability of the world's ecosystems a critical development priority for the 21st century." This volume echoes their commitment and seeks to make it a reality.

The ecosystem concept applies to modified ecosystems such as cities, farms, plantations, and reservoirs, just as much as it does to natural habi-

Box 4.2. World Resources 2000–2001 and the Pilot Assessment of Global Ecosystems

World Resources 2000–2001: People and Ecosystems, the Fraying Web of Life is published by the United Nations Development Programme, the United Nations Environment Program, the World Bank, and the World Resources Institute (WRI). It brings together information from more than 175 scientists around the world, who contributed to a pilot-scale assessment of five major ecosystem types around the world. The Pilot Assessment of Global Ecosystems (PAGE) evaluated the state of these ecosystems by examining their capacity in relation to essential goods and services, such as producing food and fiber, providing sustained flows of clean water, maintaining biodiversity, storing atmospheric carbon, and providing recreational and tourism opportunities. It included both the current level of production of these goods and services and the likely capacity of the ecosystems to produce them in the future.

The findings of the PAGE are sobering:

- Future world food production is threatened by ongoing degradation of many agro-ecosystems.
- Forest areas in some industrial countries are increasing slightly, but in developing countries, agricultural expansion, logging, and other factors are reducing forests by at least 140,000 square kilometers per year.
- Freshwater ecosystems are the most degraded of all ecosystems worldwide, and their ability to support human, plant, and animal life is greatly imperiled.
- Grassland ecosystems have declined in extent and condition and in their ability to support plant and animal life.
- Coastal and marine ecosystems are in danger of losing their capacity to provide fish, protect coastal infrastructure, reduce pollution and erosion, and sustain biodiversity.

The PAGE also produced statistics on the status and use of key environmental resources. For example, it concluded that existing fishing fleets worldwide are 40 percent larger than the ocean can sustain and nearly 70 percent of the world's major marine fish stocks are being exploited at or above their sustainable limit.

The WRI report recommends that governments and people regard the sustainability of ecosystems as essential to human life and calls for an Ecosystem Management approach to managing the world's critical resources. Specifically, decisions on land and resource use must be evaluated on the basis of how they affect the capacity of ecosystems to sustain life and to produce goods and services, both now and in the future.

tats. In all cases, diverse communities of living organisms (including human beings) rely on ecological processes such as energy, hydrological, nutrient, and mineral (including carbon) cycles to provide life essentials such as water, air, and food. Disruption or elimination of these basic ecological processes can result in a wide range of negative impacts, including soil erosion and depletion; drought or flooding; the spread of vector-borne diseases of humans, animals, and crops; and species extinctions. The devastating impact of recent floods in Mozambique, South Africa, and Zimbabwe, is believed to have been aggravated by deforestation and soil compaction in watershed areas. If the cycles and processes are disrupted on a large scale or over a long period, the ecosystem can collapse beyond the point of recoverability.

Ecosystem management is sometimes misunderstood as excluding or sidelining human activities in favor of preserving pristine nature. In fact, the essence of IEM is maintaining the capacity of ecosystems to produce environmental goods and services that are essential for life and livelihoods. Ecosystems moderate the climate; produce food, fiber, and energy; purify, store, and transport water; and recycle wastes. Human activities can in turn have profound impacts upon the biological, chemical, and physical processes that underlie these life-supporting functions. This impact can involve total transformation, as when forests are cleared for agriculture or wetlands are drained or dredged for development. It can also take the form of selective exploitation of specific products, such as particular species of timber or fish, or burning vegetation to trigger new sprouting of grasses. Past practices of modifying and managing ecosystems in this way have often further impoverished the rural poor because they lose important assets, often without sharing in whatever benefits may result (for example, see box 2.1 on the Lake Victoria ecosystem).

For the purposes of this strategy, we have coined the phrase *people-focused ecosystem management* to emphasize the fact that the IEM approach is not only about preserving natural habitats. Meeting human needs and enhancing economic production on a sustainable basis are the ultimate objectives of an IEM-based approach to development.

Integrated ecosystem management is proposed as an alternative to the conventional, sector-by-sector approach to managing natural resources, which has failed to produce sustainable results because it ignores or compromises the linkages and interactions among natural systems. Even community-based natural resource management (CBNRM), which is more cross-sectoral, still fails to deal with the full scope of the relationship between people and their environment, and the range of ecological functions and linkages that affect the production and sustainability of natural resources. CBNRM also works on a relatively small geographical scale, which is rarely sufficient to encompass ecological processes. For example, soil erosion caused by deforestation in distant watersheds can lead to siltation of lakes and rivers, and therefore to declining fish populations.

Adopting an ecosystem-based approach has some important strategic and operational implications:

- It usually involves coordinating management across relatively large landscapes, including areas and resources owned or controlled by different groups of stakeholders (often across national borders).
- It is fundamentally cross-sectoral and holistic, calling for coordination among many stakeholders.
- The objectives combine conservation and use of environmental and natural resources, which often entails compromises and tradeoffs.
- Ecosystem management requires a regular assessment of the condition of ecosystems and an understanding of the processes that sustain them and their productivity.
- Presently, however, our knowledge of ecosystem functions and the impacts of different kinds of perturbations is very limited; this calls for applying the "precautionary principle."

The "Malawi Principles" for the ecosystem approach further stress that the objectives of management of land, water, and living resources are not predetermined but are a matter of societal choice, to be determined by those directly affected (see box 4.3). Ecosystem management therefore represents integrated area and development planning, built upon a sound understanding of ecological assets and processes. Planning must be driven by communities and coordinated by local and national governments to provide the framework for integration across larger landscapes. The role of environmental agencies and specialists is to support and influence planning processes with information and analysis on environmental opportunities and constraints and on the importance of environmental goods and services that only healthy ecosystems can provide. Common entry points for the environmental agenda into these development planning processes include water resource management, soil conservation, environmental health, and tourism development.

Building an Enabling Environment for Environmental Management

In Africa, as elsewhere in the world, people and governments generally understand in principle the importance of maintaining a healthy and productive environment, yet they continue to act in ways that diminish or degrade it. This contradiction arises because the political, economic, and

Box 4.3. The Malawi Principles

1. The objectives of management of land, water, and living resources are a matter of societal choice.
2. Management should be decentralized to the lowest appropriate level.
3. Ecosystem managers should consider the effects (actual or potential) of their activities on adjacent and other ecosystems.
4. Recognizing potential gains from management, there is usually a need to understand and manage the ecosystem in an economic context. Any such ecosystem management should (a) reduce those market distortions that adversely affect biological diversity, (b) align incentives to promote biodiversity conservation and sustainable use, and (c) internalize costs and benefits in the given ecosystem to the extent feasible.
5. To maintain ecosystem services, conservation of ecosystem structure and functioning should be a priority target of the ecosystem approach.
6. Ecosystems must be managed within the limits of their functioning.
7. The ecosystem approach should be undertaken at the appropriate spatial and temporal scales.
8. Recognizing the varying temporal scales and lag effects that characterize the ecosystem processes, objectives for ecosystem management should be set for the long term.
9. Management must recognize that change is inevitable.
10. The ecosystem approach should seek the appropriate balance between, and integration of, conservation and use of biological resources.
11. The ecosystem approach should consider all forms of relevant information, including scientific, indigenous, and local knowledge; innovations; and practices.
12. The ecosystem approach should involve all relevant sectors of society and scientific disciplines.

Source: Workshop organized in Malawi in January 1998, in association with the Fourth Conference of the Parties of the Convention on Biological Diversity.

institutional environment in most countries overwhelmingly favors actions that degrade the environment rather than protect it. Environmental management is not something that can be done once and then ignored, nor can it be solely the responsibility of a few people or institutions. For a real and lasting impact, maintaining a healthy and productive environment must be everyone's goal and everyone's business. Therefore, the Bank places a high priority on creating an environment that motivates and enables a broad range of individual and institutional stakeholders to manage and protect it for the sake of their own interests.

The essential elements of an enabling environment are a broad and informed consensus on environmental and sustainable development objectives; policy, regulatory/legal, and institutional frameworks to support these objectives; and mechanisms to track results and feed them back into the decisionmaking processes. While specific needs will vary among countries, in general priority actions include the following:

- Putting in place an umbrella policy that sets out core objectives for environmentally and socially sustainable development (identified through a broad consultation process) and articulates a national commitment to them
- Harmonizing key sectoral policies with this umbrella policy, including transparent and locally accepted mechanisms for allocating ownership, access, and use rights for natural resources and other public assets
- Establishing some form of legally mandated environmental assessment requirement, including mechanisms to ensure early and effective disclosure and prior consultation with potentially affected people and other stakeholders, as well as grievance procedures
- Stocktaking of environmental assets, including economic valuation
- Building and maintaining a geo-referenced database of environmental assets and trends, including data analysis and packaging in forms that are accessible and usable by stakeholders and decisionmakers
- Creating a sound and predictable investment environment by putting in place the basic "operating rules" (for example, minimum standards for environmental quality, tax regimes, and other economic instruments) and the instruments and capacity to apply them consistently to create a predictable investment environment
- Enhancing in-country capacity to implement all the above by providing educational and training opportunities, as well as productive employment opportunities for the trained personnel.

The World Bank and other development partners have supported these types of actions in many African countries, but with limited success. In many cases the problem has been a lack of real consensus among the important actors on the tradeoffs that must sometimes be made. In reorienting our approach for greater effectiveness, we must focus on two fundamental aspects: (a) reversing the incentives that currently drive people, individually and collectively, to destroy or degrade the environment and

(b) providing the essential technical and institutional tools for environmental stewardship.

CREATING INCENTIVES FOR BETTER ENVIRONMENTAL MANAGEMENT. Incentive structures must be addressed from both ends: creating significant disincentives for environmentally unsound practices as well as concrete and meaningful rewards for good practices. The particular challenge for environmental management is that many activities that degrade the environment provide immediate, direct benefits, whereas the benefits of protecting the environment tend to be long term and diffuse. This dilemma exists regardless of whether control of the resources is in the hands of government, private companies, communities, or individuals. It represents a form of market failure, which may have to be addressed through government intervention such as subsidization.

Examples of policy measures to improve incentives for environmental management include the following:

- Eliminating direct and indirect subsidies for ecologically inappropriate activities (for example, compensation or relief for crop failure, which reduces the grower's risk; free or highly subsidized infrastructure); *conversely*, directly and indirectly subsidizing ecologically sound land uses to make them more competitive with destructive practices (for example, specialized extension or marketing services for "conservation farming")
- Eliminating policies that allow people to lay claim to public land by clearing, draining, or otherwise altering it; *conversely*, instituting policies that allow people to claim degraded land by restoring it ecologically
- Eliminating tax or other incentives that encourage environmentally damaging agricultural or industrial activities; *conversely*, providing tax and other incentives.

Aside from these indirect measures, in some cases it is appropriate to provide incentives in the form of direct payment for environmental protection services. For example, in Costa Rica the Environmental Services Payment Program pays landowners to maintain forest in critical watershed areas. Similar "land stewardship contracts" and direct payment programs are found in many countries. In the case of most developing countries, global stakeholders must be mobilized to help pay for these environmental services. This is the principle behind the Global Environment Facility, the Prototype Carbon Fund, and others. One key strategic objective is to help African countries capture a substantial share of the market for global environmental services such as biodiversity conservation and reduction of atmospheric greenhouse gases.

PROVIDING THE TECHNICAL TOOLS FOR BETTER ENVIRONMENTAL MANAGE-MENT. Better environmental management requires a number of technical tools. These tools include up-to-date and accurate information, knowledge management, economic analysis, and the appropriate technology to translate the knowledge into usable practices.

Information. Probably the most important technical tool for environmental management is up-to-date, geo-referenced data on environmental conditions and trends, analyzed and presented in a form that is relevant and usable for decisionmakers. Putting in place mechanisms to collect, process, and disseminate such information is an essential aspect of building an enabling environment. Experience shows, however, that such information systems are often "the first to go" when funds become scarce, and they typically do not survive long past the closing of the externally financed projects that supported their creation. To be sustainable, they must either become firmly institutionalized within government systems (for example, environmental laws in some countries mandate regularly updated State of the Environment Reports that require data inputs), or be strongly targeted to producing information that has a clear commercial value with willing buyers. In either case, the costs must be kept as low as possible.

Knowledge management. Information does not generate knowledge until it is verified to be accurate and is provided in a usable form. External support for environmental information often emphasizes providing state-of-the-art data management technology such as Geographic Information Systems, without adequately addressing the issue of the quality or reliability of the data being fed into it. For example, many countries do not have accurate and current local information concerning the extent, rate, and location of deforestation and forest degradation, but rely on large-scale and often outdated databases, such as the U.N. Food and Agriculture Organization's satellite-based Global Forest Resource Assessment, which provides information on a national level and is updated every 10 years. One important strategy for generating more up-to-date information on an appropriate scale is to ensure that environmental assessments undertaken for proposed development projects include thorough baseline studies. The scope of these studies should extend beyond the project site to the ecosystem scale and should cover all the elements of the ecosystem and its functions. This is one form of Strategic Environmental Assessment, which supports the ecosystem-based planning approach called for in the WRI 2000–2001 report (2000).

Economic analysis. Another area of environmental information that has received a great deal of attention by the World Bank and others is the economic valuation of environmental goods and services. Although it is important to have credible data on the current and potential economic ramifications of deforestation, soil erosion, declining fish populations,

polluted water, and the like, an overemphasis on this type of environmental economic analysis can be counterproductive. Although many valuation paradigms and models have been developed to try to capture the
broadest possible range of environmental goods and services, they cannot reflect the full value of nonmonetizable and intangible outputs of
ecosystems, such as ecological stability and resilience, as the option value
of maintaining genetic diversity. Accepting such assessments as the primary basis for decisionmaking can lead to discounting these types of values relative to other, more easily monetized ones. Furthermore, economic
value information will have an influence only if decisions are made on a
rational economic basis. Often this is not the case, as political considerations regularly outweigh strictly economic ones when it comes to resource
use and environmental management. Therefore, while economics-
related information is needed, its importance should not be overempha-
sized relative to other priorities, such as obtaining good baseline and
monitoring data on ecological resources and processes, and sociological
and political assessments that help reveal the interests of stakeholders
and the intricacies of decisionmaking processes.

Appropriate technology. Technology is often the means by which knowledge, based on research, is translated into usable tools. Many resource
users are concerned about environmental degradation and would be prepared to shift to less destructive practices if presented with viable alternatives. Barriers to the adoption of alternative technologies can include
the following:

- Higher production costs (in terms of inputs of capital, labor, land, and
  so on)
- Lower productivity
- Higher demands for knowledge and management skills
- Lack of information about the new technology
- Lack of experience and confidence in the new technology
- Custom and resistance to change.

Sometimes these barriers can be overcome through improvements in
the technology itself. In other cases they can be overcome by putting in
place positive incentives that compensate for negative ones (see box 4.4).
These incentives may be provided by the market (for example, premium
prices for organic or "green"-certified products) or through direct or indirect subsidies that serve to "internalize" the externalities of environmental degradation.

PROVIDING THE INSTITUTIONAL TOOLS FOR BETTER ENVIRONMENTAL MANAGE-
MENT. Technical solutions are often known but not implemented because

---

Box 4.4. Integrated Pest Management as an Example of Alternative Technology

Integrated Pest Management (IPM) refers to an approach in which a variety of measures are used to control the size of pest populations and reduce their negative economic or health impacts. It includes ecological manipulation aimed at making the local environment less hospitable to the survival and multiplication of the pest species and direct interventions to exclude or kill them. Synthetic chemical pesticides often represent one tool, but they are used only as a last resort when other measures fail and pest populations exceed a predetermined "economic threshold" where the benefits from treatment are expected to exceed the costs.

While IPM is practiced in many cropping and disease vector control systems around the world, its overall adoption rate remains relatively low. Some of the reasons include the following:

- Effective, reliable nonchemical pest control measures may not yet have been developed for the particular cropping system in a particular environment.
- It can require more labor and more expensive inputs (for example, selective pesticides).
- Productivity per unit of land may be reduced (for example, through the need for intercropping, crop rotation, or the use of lower-yielding crops selected for their pest resistance).
- It requires active observation and management (for example, scouting for pests, calculating thresholds).
- Far fewer promoters are disseminating information on IPM than on chemical pesticides.

Where IPM has been adopted, it has often been because there was no alternative (for example, crashes in cotton production in Texas and Mexico and rice production in Indonesia because of an explosion of pesticide-resistant pests following the destruction of natural enemies through excessive pesticide use), or because growers have been able to tap premium markets for crops grown without pesticides (for example, production of organic cotton and vegetables by smallholders in Uganda). In other cases education and awareness raising have succeeded in convincing growers that the longer-term benefits of adopting an IPM approach compensate for the short-term costs.

---

of institutional obstacles and constraints. Institutions—in the broad sense of "rules of the game" rather than just organizational structures—are the means for translating intention and policy into collective action. Despite a great deal of targeted support from the World Bank and other donors, institutional structures across the region generally remain weak and ineffective, as well as being heavily dependent on financial and technical assistance. To achieve greater and more lasting impacts in the future, we must learn from past experience and acknowledge and explicitly address a number of important "real world" constraints and obstacles, such as those outlined in table 4.2.

Aside from these long-standing and general issues, the evolving African context and new strategic approaches to environmental management in Africa present new institutional challenges, such as the following:

- Pursuing intrinsically cross-sectoral objectives within the typically sectoral organizational framework of government
- Promoting and implementing environmental management in the context of decentralization and Community-Driven Development
- Achieving cooperation and coordination in planning and implementation across political and jurisdictional boundaries
- Introducing "adaptive management" through an effective planning-monitoring-replanning cycle
- Achieving affordability and sustainability.

Mobilizing Resources for Environmental Management

Environmental management is habitually underresourced because environmental services are undervalued or treated as free goods, both in public policy and in private transactions. A key objective over the next 5 to 10 years will be to address this market distortion and generate sustainable funding for environmental management by "internalizing" environmental externalities in the form of user fees, taxes, and other economic and market-based instruments. This includes developing and capturing a substantial share of emerging markets for local and global environmental services such as water supply and purification, biodiversity conservation, and carbon sequestration.

African governments are putting a priority on reducing their dependency on international aid and increasing the role of private sector investment as an engine of economic development. The same objective must be applied to environmental management, as international aid is variable and finite and will never be adequate to meet the full scope of the needs. There is an important international trend toward increased corporate commitment to environmental stewardship and social equity, fueled in large part by consumer demand and a stronger regulatory environment. This includes cleaning up the results of past pollution; introducing more environmentally benign production methods and technologies in industry, agriculture, and energy generation; and seek-

Table 4.2. Institutional Issues and Responses

Institutional issue	Proposed strategic responses
Institutional development and capacity building is a complex undertaking that requires a sustained political and financial commitment. Often it involves fundamental changes in individual attitudes and institutional cultures. This is much harder to achieve than bureaucratic restructuring and generally takes significantly longer than expected.	Select phased programs with longer time frames. Focus explicitly on issues of institutional culture.
Institutional development and strengthening often involve loss of "turf," loss of control over valuable assets, and other threats to vested interests.	Develop an explicit strategy for "managing the losers" in any institutional change, that is, identify the interests that may be threatened and find ways to either address their concerns or neutralize their influence.
Environment is inescapably political. Natural resources are often used to obtain, reward, or demonstrate political support, and stakeholders who protest environmental degradation may be regarded as politically motivated.	Analyze and take into account the political roots and ramifications of environmental management issues when engaging in country dialogue or designing interventions.
There are no proven, universally applicable models of effective environmental institutional structures and systems to follow.	While trying to learn from the experiences of others, tailor solutions suitable to the historical, social, and political contexts of the governments and stakeholders themselves. Be aware that a certain amount of trial and error, as well as compromise (accepting less than ideal solutions), is inevitable and must be accommodated through flexible program design.

(Table continues on the following page.)

Table 4.2. (continued)

Institutional issue	Proposed strategic responses
Most African governments are still geared to a highly "command-and-control"-oriented approach to managing private sector activity, despite their general lack of capacity (and sometimes political will) to regulate it effectively. The effectiveness of environmental laws and regulations is limited by factors such as low fines and penalties, the absence of clear environmental standards, inadequate resources allocated to regulatory and monitoring functions, weak judicial systems, interference by political and other vested interests, and a generally weak "culture of compliance" with government regulations.	Encourage and assist client governments to (a) simplify and streamline regulatory systems as much as possible (focusing on those controls that give the most return per unit effort) and (b) explore alternative models based on incentives, self-regulation, and decentralized controls.
The most effective weapon against environmental degradation is a large, informed, and empowered constituency. In many countries, however, affected people are presently poorly informed or lack the means, influence, and organization to demand accountability and action.	Understand that environmental education and building stakeholder consultation into Environmental Assessments and similar processes are important, but only part of the agenda. They must be complemented by financial, technical, and policy level support to enable the various stakeholders to play their roles effectively. For example, constitutional provisions and laws that establish an individual's right to a healthy environment can enable citizens to mount legal challenges against destructive actions or misallocation of resources by private or public sector actors.
It is difficult to evaluate the progress and impact of institutional development actions. Unlike direct environmental interventions that can be evaluated in terms of	Note that monitoring and evaluation of institutional capacity-building projects must accommodate subjective forms of data and reporting (avoiding reliance solely on narrow checklists),

tangible and (in principle) objectively measurable impacts on the ground, institutional capacity-building programs tend to use process indicators. Efforts to reduce processes to outputs to provide a checklist for monitoring progress can create a misleading picture. For example, commonly used objective indicators such as the official adoption of policies, enactment of legislation and regulations, and establishment of organizational structures have little meaning without an assessment of subjective aspects such as their quality and sustainability.

use leading indicators to identify trends, and take a long-term view of visible impacts.

ing opportunities for environmentally and socially positive investments. African countries can and should benefit from this trend; they must also take measures to avoid becoming a "dumping ground" for private interests seeking to avoid responsibility and regulations imposed by other countries.

5
Implementing the Strategy

This volume will serve as a guiding framework for the World Bank's Africa Region to achieve objectives at four levels:

- Mainstreaming environment in economic development
- Building an enabling environment and strengthening environmental management capacity within the region at all levels
- Further enhancing the environmental quality of the Bank's lending operations, including both project-based and nonproject lending
- Exercising selectivity.

The Implementation Matrix (appendix A) summarizes implementation priorities based on the main strategic objectives, the urgent issues relating to them, and the desired future situation (desired outcomes). It identifies key policy and operational-level actions needed to improve environmental conditions in the short term, and to build an enabling environment for environmental management in the longer term. Progress at the regional level is to be measured in terms of the numbers or percentages of countries where such actions have been undertaken. The baseline values for these indicators (fiscal 2002 status) are to be filled in through consultation with country teams and sectoral units by June 2002. Where the information to do so credibly is lacking, either the indicator will be dropped as nonessential or work will be initiated to obtain the necessary information. The ARES Business Plan for fiscal 2002 (appendix B) follows the overall structure of the World Bank Environment Strategy, that is, categorizing objectives under the headings of Strengthen Analytical and Advisory Services, Improve Project and Program Design, Improve the Safeguard System, and Support Institutional Alignment. Under the objective "Undertake systematic monitoring and reporting on performance," the main activity will be completing the fiscal 2002 baseline indicators for the Implementation Matrix, against which future progress will be tracked.

The following sections provide the background behind the Implementation Matrix and the Business Plan.

Mainstreaming Environment in Economic Development

Mainstreaming means building environmental objectives, actions, and targets into macroeconomic and sectoral strategies and also into ("nonenvironmental") operational programs and projects. This may be regarded as a four-step process. The first step involves data collection and analysis to demonstrate and quantify the contribution of environmental resources and services to economic stability, development, and poverty alleviation, and conversely the actual and opportunity costs of continuing environmental degradation. Only when key actors and stakeholders agree on the overall objectives of environmental management and are committed to it can mainstreaming become a reality. The second step is to identify and analyze alternative development options and to identify—and, to the extent possible, quantify—the costs, benefits, and tradeoffs associated with each. The third step is to mobilize the technical and institutional tools needed to support the implementation of environmentally favorable options. Finally, the fourth step is to monitor and track impacts, based on realistic indicators, and apply principles of adaptive management to ensure continued progress toward agreed-on objectives.

Activities under the ARES for mainstreaming environment will therefore include the following:

- Developing and piloting tools and models for country-level analysis of environmental resources, trends, and conditions, with a particular emphasis on aspects directly linked to causation and alleviation of poverty. One key element is strengthening coverage of environment and natural resource issues in the analysis of the determinants of poverty in the context of Poverty Reduction Strategy Papers (PRSPs), and then in the operational strategies and programs emerging from this analysis.
- Developing and piloting tools and models for analysis and comparison of alternative economic development scenarios based on an assessment of environmentally related opportunities and constraints.
- Enhancing environmental sustainability in key sectors by identifying key environmental linkages, improving incentive structures, introducing and disseminating information, and supporting appropriate technology transfer both through direct investment and by removing barriers.
- Introducing an "integrated ecosystem management" approach, particularly in natural resource management and spatial development initiatives. In some areas this will include an emphasis on strengthening

subregional cooperation for the management of transborder resources and ecological systems.

• Developing meaningful, and piloting the use of, practical indicators for assessing environmental conditions and trends and environmentally related poverty impacts. At the program level, more objective indicators are needed to assess the extent and quality of integration of environment within sectoral strategies, project and program designs, portfolio assessments, and the like.

Consistent with regional objectives and the World Bank Environment Strategy, a primary objective will be mainstreaming environment within key strategic and planning instruments such as PRSPs and CASs. This should be reflected at the operational level in the form of environmental objectives and measures being incorporated into macroeconomic support operations such as Poverty Reduction Strategy Credits, Public Expenditure Review Credits, Structural and Sectoral Adjustment operations, and sectoral investment programs. To be able to engage meaningfully in these strategic exercises and operations, a solid groundwork must be laid in the form of up-front analytical work. To some extent this calls for targeted environmental studies, but it is equally important to ensure that relevant environmental issues are covered in other economic and sector work (ESW), including cross-cutting work such as poverty assessments.

For mainstreaming at the macroeconomic and policy levels, priority will be given to countries where the linkages between environmental action and poverty alleviation are strong and well recognized, as reflected in a willingness on the part of both the client governments and the Bank's country teams and management to support the necessary analysis and consultation processes and to incorporate the results of these processes into their strategic thinking. Other considerations include putting a priority on countries where the Bank has a strong ongoing dialogue and a substantial and diverse lending program, as these provide leverage and opportunities for engagement and action across a range of sectors and programs.

For mainstreaming at an operational level, the main targets will be multisectoral development programs, such as community- and district-level action plans and spatial development initiatives, including those involving transborder resource management and integration. Highest priority will be given to (a) opportunities to influence, from an early stage, the development of sectoral strategies and programs with a strong linkage between environmental issues and poverty impacts (for example, water resource management, energy, urban development, land redistribution); (b) situations where the policy framework provides, or may be influenced to provide, an enabling environment for local stakeholders to participate in land and resource management decisions; and (c) situations where ongoing or prospective development pressures present an urgent threat to locally and/or globally significant environmental assets and there may be an opportunity to propose more sustainable development options.

Building an Enabling Environment and In-Country Capacity for Environmental Management

As discussed above, the disappointing record on in-country institutional capacity building can and must be improved (see table 4.2). Specific actions that the Bank will take to support effective capacity building include the following:

- Building and supporting environmental constituencies, including local NGOs, professional associations, and environmentally oriented journalists; raising awareness and knowledge among political leaders and the like
- Orienting Environmental Support Programs to ensure development of broad-based capacity, including sectoral agencies, decentralized and community levels, the private sector, and civil society
- Complementing regulatory instruments with other approaches, including financial incentives, self-regulation and public/private partnership, and civil action
- Establishing sustainable subregional and regional networks and institutions to capture "efficiencies of scale" for technical fields such as EA and Environmental Information Systems
- Strengthening and supporting environmental objectives, capacity, and programs of organizations working for subregional integration and coordination
- Developing career paths and opportunities for environmental professionals in the region.

Mobilizing resources to maintain the capacity for environmental management over the long term remains one of the greatest challenges, particularly in developing countries. Key actions for the Bank are as follows:

- Building government commitment for support for environmental management by demonstrating the development and poverty linkages
- Supporting the development of mechanisms to "internalize" environmental externalities and ensure that users pay a greater part of the cost of environmental services, including both maintaining ecological functions (for example, water supply) and absorbing waste products (the "polluter pays" principle)

- Enhancing African countries' access to markets for global environmental services by helping them to identify opportunities and eliminate barriers and obstacles, and by serving as an "honest broker" to bring parties together and facilitate negotiations
- Supporting policy reforms that create an enabling environment for environmentally sound private sector investment and restricting and discouraging environmentally damaging investment
- Supporting the development of long-term financing mechanisms such as trust funds.

Enhancing the Environmental Quality of Bank Lending

Two specific aspects of environmental quality of the lending portfolio can be identified: (a) ensuring compliance with EA and other environmental and social Safeguard Policies (SPs), as well as going beyond the "do no harm" nature of the SPs to mobilize Bank lending as an active, positive force for improving environmental conditions and management; and (b) incorporating concrete objectives and targets within the logframes of Bank-financed operations, and ensuring that everything possible is done to achieve them. There is room for improvement in both of these areas. At the same time, in an environment of limited resources, quality improvement goes hand in hand with selectivity—focusing greater attention on a smaller number and range of high-priority initiatives.

Environmental Assessment and Safeguard Policies

The Bank is widely recognized, even among its critics, as a leader among bilateral and multilateral agencies with respect to its progressive and far-reaching EA requirements and its environmental and social SPs. Our application of these policies is sometimes questioned, occasionally to the extreme, when dissatisfied stakeholders bring cases to the Inspection Panel. Most criticism focuses on the implementation of the Environmental Management Plans and Resettlement Plans (and the quality of the Bank's supervision of this implementation), and on the fact that a substantial portion of our lending portfolio (particularly adjustment lending) is not covered by the EA or other SPs. These issues are regularly raised within the Bank as well as externally.

Proposed actions to improve the Africa Region's performance and impact in relation to EA and SPs include the following:

- Strengthening "ownership," both within the Bank and among our clients, by increasing awareness and knowledge not only of the contents and provisions of the Bank's environmental and social SPs but also of the reasoning and experience behind them

- Improving the integration of environmental and social assessment and mitigation, including a particular emphasis on poverty linkages
- Providing guidance for task teams on issues that frequently emerge as confusing or problematic in the application of SPs (for example, interpreting the requirements and putting in place an acceptable "Process Framework," as called for in the recently revised Involuntary Resettlement Policy)
- Increasing support for, and monitoring of, the implementation and impacts of mitigation measures identified through the EA process, as outlined in project Environmental Management Plans
- Strengthening in-country and regional EA capacity through development of policy, legislation, and institutional development; technical training; and professional networks including both public and private sector players
- Developing tools and piloting the application of "strategic" environmental assessment (SEA) tools to the Bank's "nonproject" lending instruments such as budget support (SALs, sector adjustment loans, PRSCs, PERCs), sectoral investment programs, long-term programmatic lending (for example, horizontal and vertical Adaptable Program Loans), and decentralized multisectoral operations such as Community-Driven Development initiatives and social action funds.

Quality of Design, Implementation, and Supervision of Lending Operations

A recent internal review of quality issues in Africa Region lending identified the need for an improvement in design ("quality at entry") and supervision, both for environmental projects and for environmental aspects of lending operations in general. Specifically, objectives should be more concrete and better articulated, performance indicators and targets should be more specific and measurable, and project supervision should give greater attention to reviewing and reporting on these indicators and objectives. The review also noted that risk assessments should be more frank and realistic, particularly with regard to the possible impacts of constraints such as inadequate high-level government and stakeholder commitment, lack of supporting policies, and weak institutional capacity. Task teams, country teams, and the Africa Region Environment and Social Development Unit (AFTES) have a shared responsibility for achieving these quality improvements.

Experience to date indicates the importance of moving toward longer-term, programmatic operations that combine identification of concrete, substantive goals for improving environmental quality with a flexible, "adaptive management" approach to implementation. Furthermore, Bank lending is moving increasingly toward nonproject models, including policy-based lending on the one hand, and CDD approaches, including social action funds, on the other. These more open-ended lending models and instruments call for new approaches to quality assurance, focusing on processes and impacts rather than the design and implementation of specific activities.

Exercising Selectivity

Given the scope of the environmental agenda and the large number of countries in the region, the Bank will have to exercise selectivity both in the nature of its interventions and in the countries where it concentrates its financial and human resources. In some cases this will mean that initiatives which are regarded as relatively low priority, or as unlikely to succeed given capacity, political, or other constraints, will not be undertaken. In other cases, it will mean that the Bank will seek partners to undertake initiatives that are important and timely, but for which the Bank is not the best source of support. General guidance is provided in other strategic documents, such as the Joint Operational Strategy for Biodiversity Conservation and Improved Forest Management (JOS), and the Integrated Coastal Zone Management Strategy. For example, the JOS recommends priorities for Bank involvement in the forest management sector in various countries, based on factors such as the economic and social importance of forests and their biodiversity and the suitability of the existing policy framework. Beyond this, decisions must be based on country-specific, up-front analysis of the urgency and complexity of environmental issues and the commitment and capacity to undertake them.

Many of the Bank's stakeholders and partners regard the Bank's comparative advantage as being at the level of influencing policy, both through technical assistance and dialogue and through linkage with large-scale budget support and sectoral investment programs. The role of individual investment operations is likely to decline within the Bank's portfolio over the next decade, with those that remain being placed in the context of longer-term, multidonor umbrellas such as the Comprehensive Development Framework and PRSCs.

Over the past decade GEF support has been an important catalyst for raising interest in the environmental agenda and triggering environmental investment in many countries. Until recently there has been little pressure for selectivity in the allocation of GEF resources, as there appeared to be more money available for Africa than the region could readily absorb. This is now changing, as demand for GEF resources has increased rapidly while donor commitments have not kept pace. The likely entry of other Implementing Agencies may further reduce the amount of GEF resources channeled through the Bank in the future. In addition, as outlined in the Africa Region's GEF strategy, priority is now increasingly being given to using GEF resources to support broad-based, multidonor programs, rather than stand-alone GEF or blended GEF-IDA projects.

Resources for Implementing the Strategy

Financial and technical resources for implementing the ARES are expected to come from (a) country program budgets for country-specific ESW and operations; (b) regional budget allocations for implementation of the ARES and associated environmental strategies,[9] for enhancing the understanding and application of Safeguard Policies, and for studies and other initiatives with wider regional application, such as development and testing of new methodologies and tools; (c) Bank-wide instruments such as the Mainstreaming Fund for Environment, the Institutional Development Facility, research grants, the GEF, and other multinational and bilateral trust funds; and (d) financial and in-kind support in the context of strategic partnerships.

The GEF will continue to represent an important source of support for environmental action, with an emphasis on using it strategically to maximize benefits to regional and local objectives. Regional priorities and opportunities for such local and global linkages are identified in the Bank's Strategic Frameworks and the Joint Operational Strategy for Biodiversity Conservation and Improved Forest Management in Africa, and in the Integrated Land-Water Management Action Program in Africa (ILWMAP) currently under development. The GEF Operational Program # 12 provides new opportunities to obtain GEF support for reversing land degradation trends, through an Integrated Ecosystem Management approach that links land management with biodiversity conservation and carbon storage. GEF support is also likely to be particularly helpful in facilitating transfrontier initiatives, which are becoming increasingly important with the adoption of ecosystem-level programs.

Strategic Partnerships

Strategic partnerships will be vital to the implementation of the ARES, as its challenges transcend the Bank's own capacity. Currently the Africa Region participates in several Bank-wide initiatives as well as a number of Africa-specific partnerships with a variety of development partners. Existing partnerships include the World Bank/World Wildlife Fund Forestry Alliance, the Critical Ecosystems Partnership Fund executed by Conservation International, the Soil Fertility Initiative, the Nile Basin Initiative, the Central African Regional Environmental Information Management Program (REIMP), and the Regional Program in the Traditional Energy Sector, all of which involve several international partners. In addition to traditional arrangements with bilateral donors and international NGOs, opportunities for partnerships with the private sector are likely to grow as external (or intraregional) private sector investment is becoming more significant in many African countries. At a global level the private sector is increasingly seeking to demonstrate a commitment to environmental stewardship and social equity. There are important opportunities to mobilize substantial technical and financial resources within the private sector, for technology transfer, training, EA, environmental cleanup, and program investment. Because this is a relatively new type of collaboration with the potential for conflicts of interest and other issues, the Bank will need to develop a policy framework and guiding principles for engaging in these types of partnerships.

Over time the Bank will phase out its direct participation in some of its existing partnerships as the activities they support become self-sustaining, or if it is determined that they do not make the best use of the Bank's comparative advantages or that their objectives lie outside the Bank's main priorities. Key criteria for selecting continuing and new partnerships include ensuring that they address the countries' and the Bank's strategic priorities and are in the best interests of the client, that administrative costs are minimized but fully supported, and that they are completely in accordance with the Bank's Safeguard and fiduciary policies and obligations.

Appendix A

Africa Region Environment Strategy Implementation Matrix

Objective	Key issues	Desired outcomes	Required actions		Performance monitoring[a]		
			Policy	Operational/ investment	Impact indicator	Baseline FY2002	Target FY2010
		Direct actions for environmental management					
Maintain and improve sustainable natural resource-based livelihoods	Land degradation and desertification	Erosion and degradation of arable lands reduced or halted	Land tenure reform[b]	Agricultural research and extension targeting (a) sustainable agricultural intensification and (b) management of marginal lands and soils	Number of countries with progressive land tenure policies (a) officially adopted and (b) under implementation		
		Fertility of degraded arable lands restored	Eliminate incentives and subsidies for inappropriate land use				
		Land restoration and sustainable land management articulated as an important objective in agricultural	Integrated regional planning (including land use planning), on ecosystem scale	Support for community-based land restoration action	Number of countries that have made policy reforms to reduce or remove subsidies for nonsustainable natural resource use		

		strategies and programs	Number of countries with sustainable land use as an explicit objective of agricultural policy
			Number of countries in which agricultural research and extension explicitly include sustainability objectives
Depletion or deterioration of surface water and groundwater	Rational allocation of water resources	Eliminate incentives and subsidies for inefficient and low-value water uses	Number of countries with water resource management policies that explicitly address (a)
	Efficient use or conservation of water resources	Use multi-stakeholder, Integrated Coastal Zone Management framework for all interventions	

Africa Region Environment Strategy Implementation Matrix (continued)

			Required actions		Performance monitoring[a]		
Objective	Key issues	Desired outcomes	Policy	Operational/ investment	Impact indicator	Baseline FY2002	Target FY2010
Maintain and improve sustainable natural resource–based livelihoods (continued)		Water bodies cleaned up and protected from pollution	Reorient water policy objectives from focus on delivery to focus on	Water resource assessments (cross-boundary where appropriate)	sustainable use and (b) ecological value of water		
		Sustainable management of water supply and quality articulated as an important objective of water and related policies (e.g., agriculture, energy, industry, trade)	water resource management	Efficient (water-sparing), user-controlled irrigation	Number of countries with water quality standards and regulations under implementation		
			Expand cost recovery objectives beyond supply/delivery costs to include value/opportunity costs of the water itself	Water quality monitoring	Number of countries introducing water-efficient irrigation technologies and user-group management		
				Improve wastewater treatment infrastructure			
			Establish industrial				

Number of
ongoing
transfrontier
water man-
agement ini-
tiatives

policies
requiring
water efflu-
ents to meet
suitable min-
imum quality
standards

Incorporate
transfrontier
water
resource
management
objectives
(beyond exist-
ing focus on
flow volumes
of transna-
tional rivers)

Ensure a
direct linkage
between
development
of water sup-
ply infra-
structure and
wastewater
treatment
infrastructure

Africa Region Environment Strategy Implementation Matrix (continued)

			Required actions		Performance monitoring[a]		
Objective	Key issues	Desired outcomes	Policy	Operational/ investment	Impact indicator	Baseline FY2002	Target FY2010
	Loss of productive natural ecosystems	Deforestation in priority areas slowed, halted, or reversed	Reform policies/subsidies that encourage uneconomic conversion of natural habitats and short-term exploitation of natural resources	Surveys and inventories to identify natural ecosystems of high economic value	Number of countries that have made policy reforms to reduce or eliminate subsidies for uneconomic conversion of natural habitats		
		Conversion and degradation of key rangelands slowed, halted, or reversed		Studies and assessments to clarify impacts of loss of natural ecosystems on the poor			
		Degradation of wetlands and aquatic habitats (marine and fresh water), and decline in fish populations slowed,	Decentralize and devolve natural resource ownership/management to local/community levels	Strengthen communities' capacity for sustainable natural resources management	Number of countries with proactive policies and/or programs encouraging or subsidizing maintenance of natural habitats		
			Establish				

		halted, or reversed Maintenance of productive natural ecosystems articulated as an objective both at the national level (e.g., in National Biodiversity Strategy and Action Plan) and in key sectoral policies (e.g., agriculture, water, forestry, fisheries)	legal mechanisms for establishing and protecting community reserves Subsidize landowners for maintaining natural habitats that provide social or environmental goods	Multistakeholder Integrated Coastal Zone Management initiatives	Number of countries with declining deforestation rates Number of countries with wetlands conservation policies under implementation Number of ongoing Integrated Coastal Zone Management programs
Improve environmental health	Environmentally related diseases	Reduced incidence and severity of waterborne and water-	Develop health policies that emphasize addressing	Cross-sectoral health projects (focus on reducing	Number of countries with health policies that target envi-

Africa Region Environment Strategy Implementation Matrix (continued)

| | | | Required actions | | | Performance monitoring[a] | |
| | | | | | | Baseline | Target |
Objective	Key issues	Desired outcomes	Policy	Operational/ investment	Impact indicator	FY2002	FY2010
Improve environmental health (continued)		related diseases; respiratory diseases	health problems of the poor and take a cross-sectoral approach	sources of environmental disease)	ronmental disease prevention		
				Energy projects including promotion of reduced-emissions woodstoves and alternatives to woodfuels for home use	Number of countries with declining rates of water-related disease		
			Provide subsidies to encourage adoption of alternative domestic fuels		Number of countries with declining rates of respiratory disease		
	Pollution and solid and hazardous wastes (locally significant)	Air and water pollution from major industrial point sources reduced	Transport and industrial policies to reduce toxic and particulate emissions	Transportation and industrial projects include emissions reduc-	Number of countries with air quality standards for (a) particulates and		

	(b) toxic emissions

Solid waste accumulation in urban environments reduced	Policies to enable and encourage participation of private sector and civil society in waste management	Urban projects with waste management components involving government, private sector, and end-user partnership	Number of major cities with improving air quality indicators
			Number of cities with urban waste programs involving public/private/user partnership
Biohazards contained	Develop biohazard policies and implementation measures	tion components	
		Medical waste management components in health projects, including AIDS prevention	Number of health projects that include biohazard management
Loss of traditional medicines			
Important role of traditional medicine recog-	Health policies incorporate traditional medi-	Projects to maintain and strengthen knowledge,	Number of countries with health policies

Africa Region Environment Strategy Implementation Matrix (continued)

| Objective | Key issues | Desired outcomes | Required actions | | Performance monitoring[a] | | |
			Policy	Operational/ investment	Impact indicator	Baseline FY2002	Target FY2010
Improve environmental health (continued)		nized in health sector	cine as an area for government support	effectiveness, and availability of traditional medicine	including traditional medicine		
		Important habitats and populations of medicinal plants conserved/sustainably managed	National Biodiversity Strategy/Action Plan identify areas and species of high priority for traditional medicine	Projects for protection, sustainable management, and (where appropriate) ex situ cultivation of medicinal plant and animal species	Number of programs supporting development and sustainable use of traditional medicines		
		Alternative sources of medicinal plants developed (ex situ cultivation)	Bioprospecting policies aimed at ensuring both conservation and community/national benefit	Community/private sector partnerships for developing traditional medicine technologies			
		Traditional/indigenous medical knowledge retained and disseminated					

Reduce vulnerability to climate extremes and natural disasters	High degree of climate variability (especially precipitation—droughts and flooding) and associated livelihood impacts	Climate-related livelihood risks reduced People able to cope with normal range of climate variation without severe livelihood impacts	Agricultural, land, housing, and other policies promote matching land use with land potential (e.g., discourage cultivation or building in high-risk areas; support transhumant pastoralism in arid and semi-arid areas) Agricultural policies responsive to natural climate variation (e.g., include drought management provisions to assist reduction of herds)	Development of cross-sectoral risk management strategies and climate change mitigation strategies Improved systems for climate forecasting and dissemination of forecasts to users (particularly at time frame for predicting crop growing conditions)	Number of countries with effective climate forecasting/dissemination systems Number of countries with Poverty Reduction Strategies that include mitigation of climate variation and climate change

Africa Region Environment Strategy Implementation Matrix (continued)

Objective	Key issues	Desired outcomes	Required actions		Impact indicator	Performance monitoring[a]	
			Policy	Operational/ investment		Baseline FY2002	Target FY2010
Reduce vulnerability to climate extremes and natural disasters (continued)	High human impacts of extreme climate events ("natural disasters")	Human and livelihood impacts of extreme events/natural disasters reduced	Disaster risk preparedness and management strategies. "Safety net" systems (including insurance schemes accessible to small holders) "Beyond safety net" systems to assist recovery of productive livelihoods	Disaster risk preparedness initiatives (emphasizing up-front prevention, short-term safety net, and medium- and medium-term restoration of livelihoods)	Number of countries with natural disaster risk preparedness strategies and initiatives Number of countries with climate-related "safety net" systems and/or accessible insurance schemes		

Maintain global environmental values, with equitable distribution of costs and benefits	Continuing and accelerating loss of biodiversity	Biological resources important for livelihoods and economic development maintained and sustainably managed	National Biodiversity Strategies and Action Plans prepared and adopted at senior government levels (beyond direct environmental agencies and interests)	Support (cross-sectoral, participatory) development and implementation of National Biodiversity Strategies and Action Plans based on principles of the Strategic Frameworks for Biodiversity Conservation and Improved Forest Management in Sub-Saharan Africa	Number of countries with natural resources management policies that support community-based natural resource management
	Funds available for biodiversity conservation often not used efficiently (repeating failed models; lack of monitoring feedback)	High-priority globally significant biodiversity assets identified and protected (emphasizing ecosystem/habitat-level protection, not species level)	Natural resources management policies provide incentives for sustainable use and conservation rather than short-term exploitation		Number of countries with completed National Biodiversity Strategies and Action Plans
		Strong national and local constituencies	Policies to support com-	Include biodiversity conservation components within natu-	Number of biodiversity conservation support activities designed based on the principles set

Africa Region Environment Strategy Implementation Matrix (continued)

| Objective | Key issues | Desired outcomes | Required actions | | Performance monitoring[a] | | |
			Policy	Operational/ investment	Impact indicator	Baseline FY2002	Target FY2010
Maintain global environmental values, with equitable distribution of costs and benefits (continued)		for biodiversity conservation	munity-based natural resources management Land-related and natural resources management policies explicitly articulate biodiversity conservation as an objective	ral resource-related operations (including leveraging GEF and other cofinancing)	out in the Strategic Frameworks for Biodiversity Conservation and Improved Forest Management		
Climate change and its impacts		Livelihood impacts of climate change minimized and mitigated	Agricultural and other relevant policies and strategies incorporate climate change issues	Develop cross-sectoral, participatory climate change mitigation strategies and programs	Number of countries with climate change mitigation strategies (a) prepared and (b) under		

106

Actions for building an enabling environment for environmental management

Policy framework	Current macroeconomic and sectoral policies favor short-term exploitation over sustainable management	Policy frameworks identify environmental sustainability as an objective and provide appropriate incentives	Energy policies incorporate reduction of greenhouse gas emissions as an objective and provide appropriate incentives	Sub-Saharan African countries actively engaged in reducing atmospheric greenhouse gases	Develop and implement initiatives to reduce greenhouse gas emissions	implementation
	Environmental goods and services not valued; "externali-	Real values of environmental resources captured in economic	Use "green accounting" at national level and incorporation of environmental costs and benefits		Introduce a longer time frame for country development/assistance planning and strategy—either revise Country Assistance Strategy approach or use another instrument	Number of countries with an articulated 10- to 15-year development strategy incorporating environmental sustainability objectives
						Number of country programs that

Africa Region Environment Strategy Implementation Matrix (continued)

			Required actions		Performance monitoring[a]		
Objective	Key issues	Desired outcomes	Policy	Operational/ investment	Impact indicator	Baseline FY2002	Target FY2010
Policy framework (continued)	ties" not captured	instruments (pricing and penalties)	in economic evaluation of projects and programs	(e.g., Comprehensive Development Framework)	include at least one formal environmental economic and sector work activity		
	Development planning and action proceeding without adequate knowledge of environmental assets, trends, opportunities, and constraints	Development planning based on Strategic Environmental Management Framework	Include poverty-oriented environmental analysis in Poverty Reduction Strategy Papers	Shift emphasis in investment from short-term project approach to long-term programmatic approach	Number of formal macroeconomic ESW activities integrating environmental sustainability issues in objectives and design		
			Adopt Ecosystem Management as an overall strategic framework for development planning	Use economic and sector work to identify and quantify environmental values, particularly with respect	Number of CAS, PRSP, PRSC, etc.,		

to livelihood security and quality of life for the poor

explicitly and effectively incorporating environmental issues (per the Joint Staff Assessment)

Develop area-based Strategic Environmental Management Frameworks as a key input to development planning

Number of CASs, PRSPs, PRSCs, etc. that include environmental performance indicators

Number of programmatic loans in environmental and/or natural resource areas

Number of sectoral programs explic-

Africa Region Environment Strategy Implementation Matrix (continued)

Objective	Key issues	Desired outcomes	Required actions — Policy	Required actions — Operational/ investment	Performance monitoring[a] — Impact indicator	Performance monitoring[a] — Baseline FY2002	Performance monitoring[a] — Target FY2010
Policy frame-work (continued)					itly and effectively incorporating environmental issues		
Institutional capacity[c]	Environmental issues and values not internalized by sectorally oriented institutions and actors	Sectoral institutions incorporate environmental sustainability into their mandates in principle and in practice	Development of national environmental policies with cross-sectoral orientation	Institutional restructuring and training to develop environmental capacity within sectoral, local government, community-based, and private sector institutional entities-distributed across the institution, not restricted	Number of countries with national environmental policies and strategies		
	Sectoral institutions have little technical capacity for environmental planning and management	Sectoral institutions have capacity for environmental planning and management	Elaboration of policies to promote environmentally sound private sector development		Number of countries with ongoing Environmental Support Programs (World Bank-financed or other)		
			Policy-based lending				

110

Current situation	Desired outcome	Policy/actions	Strengthening activities	Indicators
Local governments, community-level organizations, and private sector companies have inadequate capacity and lack mandate or authority for environmental management	Local governments, community-level organizations, and private sector companies have adequate capacity and mandate or authority for environmental planning and management	addresses key environmental and natural resource management issues	to an environmental "focal point"	Number of countries with a functioning environmental agency
Environmental agencies are generally politically and financially weak, dependent on external support	Environmental organizations and agencies enjoy the necessary political and financial support to be effective	Policy reforms to support and facilitate environmental action by NGOs and civil society constituencies, including property rights and/or management authority over natural resources	Strengthening of environmental agencies through enabling legislation, technical capacity building, and mechanisms for financial security, using models relevant to the country situation—special emphasis on Environmental Assessment procedures and capacity	Number of environmental agencies with a business plan to achieve independence from donor support within 15 years
Government accountability to civil	An effective, organized		Strengthening of in-	Number of operations supporting local- and community-level environmental planning and management

Africa Region Environment Strategy Implementation Matrix (continued)

| Objective | Key issues | Desired outcomes | Required actions | | Performance monitoring[a] | | |
			Policy	Operational/investment	Impact indicator	Baseline FY2002	Target FY2010
Institutional capacity (continued)	society on environmental issues is inadequate	environmental constituency demanding accountability from government		country environmental constituencies; support for development of the NGO/CBO sector	Number of Community-Driven Development programs that include (a) capacity building for environmental management at the community level and (b) community activities for improved environmental management		
	Legislation and regulations for environmental management lacking, inadequate, or not enforced (coupled with a culture of "noncompliance" with environmental requirements in public and private sectors)	Local, national, and international markets for environmental goods and services mobilized to meet costs of providing them					
		Appropriate, relevant legislation and regulations			Number of projects identified by the Africa Region		

Human
resource
capacity

Inadequate
mechanisms
and institu-
tional disin-
centives for
cross-sectoral

Institutional
mechanisms
and incen-
tives in place
to promote
cross-sectoral
thinking and
action

in place for
environmen-
tal protection
and manage-
ment, includ-
ing both
enforcement
and incen-
tives/part-
nership ele-
ments

Quality and
Knowledge
group as hav-
ing (a) inade-
quate
Environmen-
tal Assess-
ment or (b)
inadequate
implementa-
tion of En-
vironmental
Management
Plans

Number of
countries
with a strong
or growing
environmen-
tal NGO sec-
tor

Informed
and civil
society con-
stituency

Cadre of
qualified

Policies sup-
portive of
civil society
organization
and action

Public infor-
mation and
awareness
educational
and commu-
nications

Percentage of
countries
with active
programs for
training of
environmen-

Africa Region Environment Strategy Implementation Matrix (continued)

Objective	Key issues	Desired outcomes	Required actions — Policy	Required actions — Operational/investment	Performance monitoring[a] — Impact indicator	Performance monitoring[a] — Baseline FY2002	Performance monitoring[a] — Target FY2010
Human resource capacity (continued)	thinking and action	environmental specialists in public and private sector (inside and outside dedicated environmental organizations)	Government commitment to support environmental policy and regulatory institutions	campaigns (informal education)	tal professionals		
	Inadequate knowledge or appreciation of the importance of environmental management among the general public			Improved coverage of environment in formal education at all levels	Number of countries with an increase in the annual number of (a) diplomas and (b) postgraduate degrees awarded by in-country institutions		
	Lack of qualified environmental specialists		Legislative and regulatory framework that establishes responsibility of private sector for its environmental impacts and performance	Strengths-weaknesses-opportunities-threats analysis to identify human resource strengthening needs (public and private sectors)			

| Environmental information and knowledge management | Inadequate baseline information on environmental resources and ecological processes

Lack of useful, practical environmen- | Up-to-date, geo-referenced data on environmental resources and trends, analyzed and presented in forms useful to decision-makers | Incorporation of environmental quality and management indicators into national development planning and monitoring (and assistance programs) | Strengthened local technical and professional training institutions (universities, etc.)

Targeted technical and professional training support for individuals (not restricted to government)

Programmatic (long-term) support for environmental survey and monitoring | Number of countries with actively managed geo-referenced environmental databases developed

Number of functioning |

115

Africa Region Environment Strategy Implementation Matrix (continued)

Objective	Key issues	Desired outcomes	Required actions		Performance monitoring[a]		
			Policy	Operational/ investment	Impact indicator	Baseline FY2002	Target FY2010
Environmental information and knowledge management (continued)	tal quality indicators	Demand-driven production and dissemination of environmental information products (used by diverse public and private sector users)			regional networks for environmental information		
	Lack of useful, sustainable environmental monitoring systems						
	Inadequate knowledge and appreciation among the general public of the importance of environmental quality and ecosystem functions	Well-educated public mobilized as an effective environmental constituency			Number of operations with components to enhance incorporation of environmental information in development planning and decisions		
	Inadequate exchange of	Functioning regional net-					

environmental information at technical and political levels

works of environmental specialists (in various specialties, e.g., environmental economics, environmental law, environmental information systems, etc.)

Key environmental issues incorporated into international diplomatic interactions and negotiations

Note: NGO = nongovernmental organization; CBO = community-based organization.

a. These indicators are to track progress at a regional level; individual country strategies will have country-specific indicators.

b. May include individual land titling or alternative community-based tenure schemes more suitable to some lifestyles or production systems (for example, pastoralism).

c. Refers not only to organizational structures and entities but to all aspects of "the rules and means of the game," legislation and regulations, organizational structure, and financial sustainability.

Appendix B

Africa Region Environment Strategy Business Plan FY2002/2003: Activities and Monitoring Matrix

Objectives	FY2002/2003 activity	Monitoring and reporting indicators
	Country level	
Strengthen country-level environmental analysis and advisory activities to inform country dialogue (e.g., country diagnostic studies)	Country environmental diagnostic studies for mainstreaming environment in Country Assistance Strategy (CAS) Countries: • Benin (CAS) • Madagascar (natural disasters) • Democratic Republic of Congo	• Number of countries with formal environmental economic and sector work (ESW) • Number of papers produced • Number of CASs reflecting environment input
Strengthen analytical work on poverty-environment linkages and inputs to Poverty Reduction Strategy Papers (PRSPs)	Mainstream environment in PRSP process. Countries: • Nigeria • Zambia • Benin (Public Expenditure and Reform Adjustment Credit)	• Number of papers produced • Number of PRSPs with mainstreaming of environment • Summary review of completed and ongoing PRSPs (update)
Identify priority cross-sectoral issues and use Strategic Environmental Assessments (SEAs) more systematically to	Identify potential SEAs Participate in SEA Countries: • Tanzania (mining)	• Number of SEAs identified • Number of SEAs completed or ongoing

influence planning and
decisionmaking processes early

- Nigeria (transport)

Regional level

Strategy development and
supporting analytical work

Completion, dissemination, and main-
streaming of regional strategies
- Africa Environment Strategy
- Biodiversity Strategic Framework
- Improved Forest Management
- Integrated Coastal Zone Management
  (ICZM)
- African Land and Water Management
  Initiative (ALWMI)
- Sustainable Rural Energy
- Forestry Management/Biodiversity
  Joint Operational Strategy

Background studies and analyses
- "Framework" paper on applying
  Integrated Ecosystem Management
  approach to natural resource
  management in Africa
- Study on opportunities and constraints
  to enable Sub-Saharan Africa to benefit
  from emerging global market in carbon
  emissions reductions and carbon
  sequestration (through Clean
  Development Mechanism)

Dissemination and outreach of regional
strategies and related analytical pieces
- Completed studies
- Published papers
- Presentations to diverse audiences
- Training workshops held

119

Activities and Monitoring Matrix (continued)

Objectives	FY2002/2003 activity	Monitoring and reporting indicators
	• Case study on integration of traditional medicine in public health systems • Monitoring and evaluation: concept paper on establishing pragmatic indicators for impacts on environmental quality Support client initiatives • Support and participate in preparations for the World Summit on Sustainable Development • Support mainstreaming of environmental sustainability in the New Partnership for African Development (NEPAD), and support development of the NEPAD Environment Initiative	
Improve the performance and development effectiveness of environment projects and programs	• Incorporate integrated ecosystem management approach in at least three projects • Integrate environment in Community-Driven Development (CDD) operations	• Number and status of projects with Integrated Ecosystem Management approach • Number of CDD operations incorporating environmental capacity building and activities
Mainstream environment into sector programs and portfolios	• Sector strategies and assessments (water, rural, land policy, community-based biodiversity management), e.g., Malawi land reform • Mainstream responses to environmental risks and natural disasters: projects and	• "Portfolio review" of sector strategies in two key sectors • Number of projects that include specific components to reduce vulnerability

	planning (infrastructure, watershed protection, land use planning)—use of EA process and other tools to introduce these elements; climate forecasting and early warning; safety nets and post-disaster rehabilitation	
Maximize synergies between local, regional, and global priorities	• African Land and Water Management Initiative (ALWMI) • Include global biodiversity components in natural resource and other related projects • Africa Stockpile Program (obsolete pesticides) • Support for development and implementation of biodiversity strategies and plans and improved forest management in Sub-Saharan Africa	• Implementation of ALWMI • Number of biodiversity components in projects • Program launch
Strengthen the implementation of safeguard policies	• Implementation Review of OP4.09 (Pest Management policy)	• Review completed
Work with clients and other development institutions to review and strengthen client safeguard capacity and harmonize safeguard procedures	• Regional Capacity Building Program for Environmental Assessment • Strengthen partnerships with regional networks • Pilot decentralization of safeguards review to South African Institute	• Number of training courses • Number of projects reviewed with SAIEA

Activities and Monitoring Matrix (continued)

Objectives	FY2002/2003 activity	Monitoring and reporting indicators
	of Environmental Assessment (SAIEA)	
Improve incentives and mechanisms for work on cross-sectoral activities and policy issues	• Increase participation of environmental staff in multisectoral teams	• Number of teams identified and activities undertaken
Strengthen World Bank Africa Region capacity in urban and industrial environment	• Recruit "brown" environment specialist	Recruitment
Leverage the role of institutional engagements and partnerships to support implementation of the Environment Strategy	Maintain and strengthen partnerships, e.g.: • Critical Ecosystems Partnership Fund (CEPF) • World Wildlife Fund/World Bank forestry initiative • Africa Stockpile Program (ASP)	• Status reports
Undertake systematic monitoring and reporting on performance	• Periodic review of Implementation Matrix and Business Plan	• Collect baseline information for indicators column of Africa Region Environment Strategy Implementation Matrix (data for FY 2002/2003) • Monitoring of Business Plan indicators

Notes

1. The World Bank has strategies and programs in the areas of population, conflict and postconflict, and HIV/AIDS.

2. With the exception of South Africa, which accounts for approximately 0.8 percent of global carbon dioxide emissions.

3. Center for Research on Epidemiology of Disasters and the Office of U.S. Foreign Disaster Assistance (CRED/OFDA), as cited in World Bank (2000e).

4. See MDG website http://www.developmentgoals.org/goals-environ.html.

5. There are some exceptions, such as Botswana, which has strict policies and priorities for water allocation and management.

6. The World Bank supported the establishment of industrial parks with appropriate wastewater treatment facilities as one response to this problem.

7. For further information, see the Global Compact homepage at http://www.un.org/partners/business/gcevent/second_page.htm.

8. GOPA Consultants. May 2001. Mainstreaming Safeguard Policy Compliance within Community-Driven Development Initiatives (CDDs) in World Bank-Funded Operations. Unpublished final report for the World Bank

9. Njie, Ndey-Isatou. "Report of ESP Study." Draft report, April 2000.

10. Also based on extensive consultations with clients, stakeholders, and development partners in-country, as well as World Bank management and staff.

References

Consultative Group on International Agricultural Research. 2000. "News from Future Harvest." *CGIAR News*, June 2000, Washington, D.C.: CGIAR.

Council on Environmental Quality. 1993. "Ecosystem Approach to Management and Biodiversity." *24th Annual Report of the Council on Environmental Quality*. Washington, D.C.: Government Printing Office.

Diamond, J. 1997. *Guns, Germs and Steel: The Fates of Human Societies*. New York: W. W. Norton & Co.

Ekbom, A. and J. Bojo. 1997. *Mainstreaming Environment in Country Assistance Strategies*. AFTE1 Discussion Paper No. 1. Washington, D.C.: World Bank.

Global Compact Homepage: http://www.un.org/partners/business/gcevent/second_page.htm.

International Federation of Red Cross and Red Crescent Societies. 1993. *World Disasters Report/International Federation of Red Cross and Red Crescent Societies*. Dordrecht, Netherlands: Nijoff.

Janowiak, J. E., and P. Xie. 1999. "CAMS-OPI: A Global Satellite-Rain Gauge Merged Product for Real-Time Precipitation Monitoring Applications." *Journal of Climate* 12 :3335–42.

The Little Green Data Book 2000. 2000. Washington, D.C.: World Bank.

Mercier, J. 1995. *Environmental Assessment and Review in Sub-Saharan Africa*. Washington, D.C.: World Bank.

Millennium Development Goals website: http://www.development goals.org/Environment.htm.

Murray, C., and A. Lopez, eds. 1996. *The Global Burden of Disease: A Comprehensive Assessment of Morality and Disability from Disease, Injuries, and Risk Factors in 1990 and Projected to 2020.* Cambridge, Mass.: Harvard University Press.

Niles, J. Forthcoming. "Tropical Forests and Climate Change." In S. H. Schneider, A. Rosencranz, and J. Niles, eds., *Climate Change Policy: A Survey.* Washington, D.C.: Island Press.

Oldeman, L.R., R. T. A. Hakkeling, and W. G. Sombroek. 1990. *World Map of the Status of Human-Induced Soil Degradation. Global Assessment of Soil Degradation (GLASOD).* Wagneningen: International Soil Reference and Information Centre and United Nations Environment Programme.

Sharma, N. P., D. Torbjorn, E. Gilgan-Hunt, and D. Grey. 1996. *African Water Resources: Challenges and Opportunities for Sustainable Development.* World Bank Technical Paper 331. Washington, D.C.: World Bank.

Shilling, J. D. 2001. *OED IDA Review Environmental Sustainability Issues in IDA 10-12.* Background Paper. Washington, D.C.: World Bank.

Shyamsundar, P., Kirk Hamilton, Lisa Segnestam, Maria Sarraf, and S. Fankhauser. 2001. *Country Assistance Strategies and the Environment.* Environment Department Papers No. 81. Washington, D.C.: World Bank.

World Bank. 1993. *World Development Report: Investing in Health.* Washington, D.C.: World Bank.

————. 1994. *Africa Can Compete! A Framework for World Bank Group Support for Private Sector Development in Sub-Saharan Africa.* Washington, D.C.: World Bank.

————. 1996. *Toward Environmentally Sustainable Development in Sub-Saharan Africa: A World Bank Agenda.* Development in Practice Series. Washington, D.C.: World Bank.

————. 1998. *World Resources, 1998–99 A Guide to the Global Environment.* New York: Oxford University Press.

————. 2000a. *Can Africa Claim the 21st Century?* Washington, D.C.: World Bank.

————. 2000b. *Cities in Transition: A Strategic View of Urban and Local Government Issues, Executive Summary.* Washington, D.C.: World Bank.

————. 2000c. *Donor Survey of Environmental Aid Effectiveness.* Environmental Strategy Background Paper. Washington, D.C.: World Bank.

————. 2000d. *Fuel for Thought: An Environmental Strategy for the Energy Sector.* Washington, D.C.: World Bank.

————. 2000e. *Intensifying Action Against HIV/AIDS in Africa: Responding to a Development Crisis.* Washington, D.C.: World Bank.

————. 2000f. *Natural Disaster Risk Management: Portfolio Review 1980–1999.* Disaster Management Facility, Washington, D.C.: World Bank.

————. 2000g. *World Development Indicators.* Washington, D.C.: World Bank.

World Health Organization. 1999. *World Health Report 1999: Making a Difference.* Paris, France: World Health Organization.

World Resources Institute. 1999. *World Resources Report, 1998–99.* Washington, D.C.: World Resources Institute.

World Resources Institute, United Nations Development Programme, United Nations Environment Programme, and the World Bank. 2000. *World Resources 2000-2001: People and Ecosystems, the Fraying Web of Life.* Washington, D.C.: World Resources Institute.